Science and Spirit

Exploring the Limits of Consciousness

CHARLES F. EMMONS
AND
PENELOPE EMMONS

iUniverse, Inc.
Bloomington

Science and Spirit
Exploring the Limits of Consciousness

iUniverse books may be ordered through booksellers or by contacting:

iUniverse
1663 Liberty Drive
Bloomington, IN 47403
www.iuniverse.com
1-800-Authors (1-800-288-4677)

ISBN: 978-1-4759-4262-0 (sc)
ISBN: 978-1-4759-4264-4 (hc)
ISBN: 978-1-4759-4263-7 (ebk)

Library of Congress Control Number: 2012914315

Printed in the United States of America

iUniverse rev. date: 08/20/2012

In memory of Jack McNab

Contents

Acknowledgments xi

Introduction xiii

We state our intentions for investigating and combining various scientific frameworks on consciousness and survival. Methodologies include ethnographic interviews with scientists, observations at conferences, and visits to research institutes.

PART ONE: THE QUESTIONS

Chapter One: What Inexactly Are the Questions? 1

It is difficult to define consciousness and to know what exactly the survival of death might involve.

Chapter Two: Why Would We Ask These Questions? 3

Various cultures see consciousness and survival differently. Chinese take ghosts and spirit mediums for granted within ancestor worship. In the West, mainstream scientists are reluctant to study these phenomena, but to most Americans, based on their experience, "The paranormal is normal."

Chapter Three: What's Science Got to Do with It? 7

Parapsychology is a threat to normal-science paradigms. Is materialistic science moving toward studying consciousness? Do people with a spiritual perspective care about science?

Chapter Four: Who's Going to Pay for This?.. 13
Normal-science funding is seldom available for studying anomalies, because "science is power." However, there are private sources, and breakthroughs are occurring especially in medicine.

PART TWO: HOW WE THINK WE KNOW WHAT WE THINK WE KNOW 19

Chapter Five: Skepticism, Ridicule, and Smart-Ass Journalism............ 21
Skepticism is necessary for science, but in excess it thwarts the goals of ideal science. Examples are given of how superskepticism operates as a social control system, even within parapsychology.

Chapter Six: There's Nothing Like an Experience................................. 37
Scientists who dare to study the paranormal have often been motivated to do so because of personal experience, which is arguably more convincing than research findings.

Chapter Seven: Subjectivity 47
When confronted with the "hard problem" (consciousness), sometimes subjective reports provide valuable insights. "Objectivity" is not enough.

Chapter Eight: A Gallery of Frames.. 54
Goffman's concept of "frame" is applied to questions of consciousness. Appreciating other frames can be difficult, and rejecting other frames can be a political strategy.

PART THREE: TYPES OF EVIDENCE 63

Chapter Nine: Consciousness 65
"Objective" science can't find our consciousness, making it the "hard problem" in neuroscience. Is our subjective consciousness merely a social construction and a personal illusion then?

Chapter Ten: OBEs and NDEs 76
Do out-of-body experiences and near-death experiences provide evidence that consciousness can exist apart from the brain? Or could it be that our awareness can be elsewhere without actual physical presence?

Chapter Eleven: Lucid Dreaming 84
Lucid dreams may be related to OBEs. Some see them as tools of self-awareness. Perhaps neuroscience can use them to study the nature of consciousness.

Chapter Twelve: ESP and Remote Viewing 92
A little history of the study of psi in general, including ESP in particular. What types of evidence are there? Is it really perception, or just nonlocal consciousness?

Chapter Thirteen: Ghosts or Apparitions 102
Ghost experiences occur similarly in all societies but with cultural variation. Various theories are considered. Are they physical at all, and do they represent surviving consciousness?

Chapter Fourteen: Physical Effects (PK, Healing) 113
Apart from physical effects associated with hauntings, we consider people's psychokinetic (PK) experiences as well as healing. Does this involve physical energy from the body or some kind of entanglement at a distance?

Chapter Fifteen: Spirit Mediumship 125
    Some consider mediumship the best evidence for survival.
    However, apart from fraud and other mundane explanations,
    how could we tell the difference from clairvoyance and
    telepathy? What do mediums think?

Chapter Sixteen: Reincarnation... 136
    Reincarnation is debated in both science and religion.
    Stevenson's evidence is "suggestive." Maybe there's nothing
    like an experience.

PART FOUR: MAKING SOMETHING OF IT................................... 147

Chapter Seventeen: Practical Applications........................... 149
    Apart from all the theoretical considerations, people find uses
    for the alleged mysteries of consciousness in a variety of
    mind/body/spirit applications.

Chapter Eighteen: Summing Up and Looking to the Future................ 154
    After recapping different "frames" on consciousness and
    survival, we give our bottom-line thoughts on the subject.

Bibliography.. 165

Index... 175

Acknowledgments

We thank many organizations and people, living and "dead", for their information and inspiration. Some people wish to remain anonymous. Special thanks to Gettysburg College and the Faculty Development Committee for funding this study.

Thanks to The Anomalous Experiences Research Unit (AERU) in Sociology at The University of York (UK), The Association for Research and Enlightenment (A.R.E.), Exploring the Extraordinary (UK), The First Spiritualist Church of Erie, The Institute of Noetic Sciences (IONS), Lily Dale Assembly, The Monroe Institute, and The Society for Scientific Exploration.

Thanks to Frederick (Skip) Atwater, Patty Ray Avalon, Stephen Braude, Doug Burns, Madeleine Castro, Laine Crosby, John Fleming (deceased), Anne Gehman, Hannah Gilbert, Garrett Husveth, James McClenon, Jack McNab (deceased), Sarah Metcalf, Darlene Miller, Mark Nesbitt, Carol Nesbitt, Lorna Prime, Paul Rademacher, Dean Radin, Al Rauber, J.B. Rhine (deceased), Serena Roney-Dougal, Leo Sprinkle, Frank Takei, Michelle Takei, Russell Targ, Lynda Terry, Brad Terry, Robert Waggoner, Robin Wooffitt, and many more.

Introduction

It is hard to imagine not being curious about our own consciousness and about what happens to that consciousness after we die. What does science have to say about consciousness, if anything? Or are these unanswerable questions relegated to religious faith and popular culture? Some of the alleged phenomena that might suggest consciousness beyond or apart from a living body are ESP, out-of-body experiences (OBEs), near-death experiences (NDEs), reincarnation, spirit mediumship, and ghost (apparition) experiences.

In the past I have written as a sociologist/anthropologist about ghosts (Chinese Ghosts and ESP, 1982), UFOs (At the Threshold, 1997), and spirit mediums (Guided by Spirit: A Journey into the Mind of the Medium, 2003, with my wife Penelope Emmons). Unlike most sociologists and anthropologists studying the "paranormal," I actually admit that I'm curious about whether such things are "real," instead of just examining other people's beliefs and experiences. Worse yet, I've even participated in the experiences, like becoming a spirit medium.

Sociology contributes to understanding "reality" by exposing the way social groups construct reality (based on social norms about how to talk and think). Exploring this social construction of reality is very subversive, and it can even end up "deconstructing" mainstream science (including social science). I will end up arguing later that scientific "objectivity" is largely a myth, and that my subjective participation as a spirit medium, for example, helps me to understand the phenomenon better.

Am I biased? Of course, but so are all scientists, and they need to expose their own biases, or have them exposed for them by others. There are many different kinds of bias to be exposed in this book when it comes to conversations about consciousness. Rather than ridiculing these biased perspectives, however, I intend to give them a sympathetic reading, to help us all understand them better, and to compare them for greater insights.

A nicer way to put this is that there are many different "frames" (or paradigms) people use for talking about consciousness and life after death: neuroscience, parapsychology, religion/spirituality, psychology, philosophy, sociology etc. Often people, including scientists, wear blinders, ignoring or disrespecting frames other than their own. As a sociologist who has the frame of studying frames, I intend to show what we can learn from a holistic, comparative view. You may be surprised.

Back to the unspoken sociological (and general scientific) taboo against caring about whether paranormal phenomena actually exist (not to mention participating in them). I care not only about the frames people use to make sense of the world, but also about what is actually in the frames. I think that a comparative, holistic study of consciousness (which may be completely "normal" . . . or not) and of consciousness apart from living bodies (which is generally considered "paranormal" of course) can be very enlightening.

Again, who is not curious about consciousness (including, I should hope, sociologists)? For quite some time inquiring about the nature of consciousness was considered fruitless in science (particularly in psychology). Advancements in neuroscience have helped change that. Nevertheless, many (most? all?) things about consciousness are still a mystery. Why should the mysterious aspects be ignored or simply associated with "trivial," sensationalized mass-media treatments of phenomena that appear to be paranormal?

One major part of our research for this book was twenty formal, depth ethnographic interviews, mostly with scientists (but also with some "real folks"), about what would be (or is) scientific evidence for consciousness apart from the body, and/or for life after death (called "survival" in parapsychology, which is the study of "psi" or psychic phenomena). I also did participant observation at meetings of the Society for Scientific Exploration (of which I am a member), at which consciousness studies are a prominent topic, and observed and engaged in many informal conversations with paranormal researchers interested in scientific methodologies. Penelope and I visited research centers and institutes such as The Monroe Institute (TMI), the Institute of Noetic Sciences (IONS), the Association for Research and Enlightenment (A.R.E.), and the Anomalous Experiences Research Unit (AERU), a graduate-level program in sociology at the University of York, England.

In this book there is not enough room for a detailed evaluation of evidence or thorough review of the literature on all the subtopics of consciousness and the paranormal, nor do I attempt to give one. I do give interesting cases to illustrate, and I guide you to important literature that you can explore in depth for yourself. My main focus is to identify the major frames and issues within them. I also tell you what I make of it all by the end. And I'm sure you will construct your own frame as well. That's called independent thinking.

My wife Penelope Emmons (a licensed counselor, ordained minister and spirit medium) also contributes to this volume by presenting her own views, especially on spirit mediumship, and reflecting on her own bottom-line conclusions at the end. Penelope helped in some of the interview sessions as well. She was an important contributor to our book *Guided by Spirit* (Emmons and Emmons, 2003), and as an intuitive she is a good counterbalance to my mostly academic point of view. But there is also a little bit of yin in the yang and yang in the yin as we have learned to trade frames.

Charles F. Emmons

PART ONE

THE QUESTIONS

Chapter One

WHAT INEXACTLY ARE THE QUESTIONS?

As in most scientific research and, as philosophers will tell you, in clear thinking in general, the most important step is to define the question clearly. I'm asking two questions: what evidence is there for consciousness apart from the body, and what evidence is there for the survival of consciousness after bodily death? I must admit that these questions are very difficult to clarify.

To begin with, what exactly is consciousness? Several times my review of the literature on the subject came across statements like, "Science has no clue about what consciousness is, or how to locate it in the brain." This could be a problem.

I remember at one meeting of the Society for Scientific Exploration, a highly respected member who had researched the mysteries of consciousness for decades stood up and chided (or perhaps commiserated with) fellow members by pointing out how the term "consciousness" was being used in so many different ways that we didn't really seem to know what we were talking about. Is it awareness, self-awareness, being awake rather than unconscious, some transcendental mystical state, or what?

And yet we all know when we are conscious. We may not know what it is, but we know when we've got it (or when we're "conscious" of it). Right now, I am conscious of myself typing on a MAC. Wouldn't you think that with all of our modern neuroscience somebody could explain how I know that, and how I know that I know that? It's maddening and fascinating at the same time. There's a lot more like this, just wait.

Another major issue has to do with what we mean by "survival after death." How would we know if Uncle Harry's "spirit" survived death? Or rather, what would we mean by saying that his spirit survived (how we would know it is another tough issue, as you will see later on)? Would he have to remember his life and identity as Uncle Harry? If he has no memory or sense of self, and he reincarnates as little Susie Q., in what sense is that a surviving Uncle Harry?

As it turns out, there are really a number of interconnected and inexact questions involved in the subject area of consciousness and whether it can exist apart from or beyond a living body. As noted in the Introduction, some of the reported phenomena that suggest consciousness beyond the body are ESP (or psi, for psychic phenomena in general), OBEs, NDEs, reincarnation, spirit mediumship, and apparition (ghost) experiences. All of these phenomena have been variously explained in different scientific frames as nonexistent, as misinterpreted normal events, as evidence for survival after death, or as evidence for psi but not necessarily for survival.

Chapter Two

WHY WOULD WE ASK THESE QUESTIONS?

In the introduction I said that it was hard to imagine people not being curious about consciousness and about whether consciousness (or spirit) survived death. I was being a bit ethnocentric when I wrote that; in other words, I wasn't taking into account cultural variations worldwide or even within the United States. As a sociologist and anthropologist I actually know better, having encountered points of view all the way from traditional Chinese who have taken the afterlife of their ancestors for granted to some mainstream scientists in Western society whose attitude seems to be, "Why are people so silly as to believe in survival?" In other words, some people's answer to "Why would we ask these questions?" is, "We wouldn't."

Of course religion has a lot to do with how people understand or question consciousness and survival. In the research I did in Hong Kong for the book *Chinese Ghosts and ESP* (Emmons, 1982), most people took the existence of ghosts for granted and sometimes minded being asked whether they believed in them ("Why do you ask me about such unlucky things?!"). Chinese ghosts are considered very unlucky or dangerous if they are not worshipped properly.

Amazingly, 72% in my random-sample survey of the residents of modern Hong Kong still practiced ancestor worship in 1980. Worshipping ones ancestors (ones ghostly relatives) rests on the assumption that they live an afterlife similar to this one and require symbolic objects or effigies of practical things like money and material goods to be sent to them by burning the effigies. People go to spirit mediums to find out what their ancestors want. This is very practical, because the living help the dead in return for favors in their own lives, in terms of health and wealth.

One day I was sitting in the waiting room of a very popular spirit medium in Hong Kong, waiting for a reading. All the others in the room were Chinese women, who started gossiping about me in Cantonese (which they never dreamed a foreigner like me could understand). Some of them recognized me as having been there before, and they had eavesdropped on my previous readings, a common practice. "Here comes the Westerner again [me] to chit-chat with his auntie!" In other words, I was being ridiculed for just "visiting" with my dead aunt through the spirit medium, instead of asking important questions like, "Did you like the [Mercedes] Benz effigy I burned for you last week?" and "Will you help me win the housing lottery?"

Aside from ancestor worship there are other Chinese traditional religious perspectives, which also take for granted survival of consciousness after death, but that are not necessarily consistent with ancestor worship. Some spirit mediums in Hong Kong who are also Buddhists hesitate to try to contact spirits who have died long ago, saying that they have probably reincarnated already.

In addition, some forms of Buddhism and other Asian religious traditions emphasize less of an individual consciousness and more of a communal afterlife (Moreman, 2006: 36-37), at least between incarnations. Rao (2002: 216-304) says that Eastern religions tend to conceive of pure consciousness, without any thought content, which of course violates both Chinese and Western assumptions about surviving consciousness with a self attached (like Uncle Harry).

Usually we think of the dominant Western way of thinking to be science, and mainstream science seems to be agnostic at best when it comes to paranormal consciousness and a spirit world. However, the situation is complicated. When it comes to paranormal aspects of consciousness, individual scientists are more accepting than you would think. Mayer (2007, 229-230) refers to a survey of 1,100 college professors in which 55% of natural scientists, 66% of social scientists, and 77% in the arts/humanities/

education thought that the existence of ESP was already established or at least likely.

However, survival is even harder to swallow than ESP from a scientific perspective, and it receives less support. Blackmore (2006: 8) noted that most of the prominent researchers in the field of consciousness studies she interviewed at a conference did not believe in life after death. And as we shall see later, mainstream science as an institution (no matter what individual scientists think) is unlikely to fund studies of paranormal consciousness, whether it involves survival or not.

Just because scientific willingness to investigate these subjects is lacking, that doesn't mean, however, that most Westerners are disinterested or disbelieving. Most Americans report having had a psychic experience (Targ, 2004: xxiv). As Andrew M. Greeley (1991: 367-374) says, "The paranormal is normal." Opinion polls have also found a majority in the U.S. believing in life after death (Storm and Thalbourne, 2006: 6; Blackmore, 2006: 8), although it is only about 25% in some European countries.

Beauregard and O'Leary (2007: 5) ask the interesting question, "Why hasn't materialism killed belief?" In other words, why hasn't the dominant scientific view, that everything obeys natural physical laws, convinced the general population that paranormal/spiritual phenomena either do not exist or are unknowable? One reason, no doubt, is that, as Greeley (1991) pointed out, most people think that they have had a paranormal experience. The answer to this is complex, but for our purposes it is sufficient to note that there is disagreement within this culture, as well as among international cultures, about how or even whether to ask questions about consciousness and survival.

Why and how we ask these questions, even in parapsychology, which has been more willing than most of mainstream science to investigate consciousness, has changed over the past century and a half in the U.S. Scott Rogo (1979: 59-60) points out that the case of the Fox Sisters in the mid-nineteenth century was the first investigation of spirit mediumship that saw it in terms of "spirits of the dead" rather than demons. Even today the mediumistic activities of Spiritualists are sometimes condemned by conservative Christians as demonic. Rogo also identifies elements of witchcraft beliefs and demonic possession in claims of the paranormal among Roman Catholic saints and in other early spirit possession (or poltergeist) cases. And since the 1930s parapsychology has moved more into the laboratory and has relatively deemphasized both the study of apparently spiritual/religious phenomena, like spirit mediumship and hauntings, and the spiritual interpretation of these phenomena.

In this chapter we have seen perspectives or "frames" ranging from the traditional Chinese assumption that an afterlife is taken for granted and doesn't need to be questioned, to the modern mainstream scientific point of view that everything obeys material, physical laws, and therefore it is pointless to ask about a nonmaterial afterlife. Somewhere in the middle are those, including parapsychologists, who entertain the possibilities of both consciousness beyond the body and the survival of consciousness after death, and who attempt to investigate them scientifically.

So, for the people who are willing to ask such questions, what makes you think that science can answer them?

Chapter Three

WHAT'S SCIENCE GOT TO DO WITH IT?

It is easy to find authors who say that mainstream scientists are unwilling or unable to deal with questions of consciousness and survival (e.g., Becker, 1993: 1). Science writer Rita Carter (2002: 6-7) wrote at one point that conventional psychology had tended to ignore "the hard problem" (consciousness), and that no one knows "the secret of consciousness," even assuming that it is a normal scientific phenomenon.

When allegedly paranormal aspects of consciousness are considered, the resistance from mainstream science can be even greater. James McClenon (1984: 68) stated that paranormal phenomena are considered a priori impossible because they cannot be given a reductionist explanation, or broken down into simple observable physical actions in a laboratory, and therefore parapsychology is "doomed to remain a pseudoscience" (in the eyes of the scientific establishment). For example, we may be able to observe a subject (A) in a parapsychology lab making a high level of correct guesses about the pictures that someone else (B) down the hall is selecting from a larger sample of pictures, but we cannot (yet) find a mechanism for how that information is shared between A and B.

There is also a political aspect to this, because even though parapsychology uses a scientific orientation, its experimental data threaten the "metaphysical foundations of science" (McClenon, 1984: 195). This is because psi phenomena, such as allegedly being able to predict numbers produced by a random-number generator, make no sense in terms of normal-science paradigms. As one scientist reportedly said, "These are things I wouldn't believe even if they were true." Or, as I like to characterize this overly skeptical point of view, "It can't be, therefore it isn't."

I have a thought experiment to illustrate the point of how "paranormal" phenomena (or "anomalies") are treated in mainstream "normal" science. I ask students in my Gettysburg College class "Science, Knowledge and the New Age" to imagine what would happen if they attended a Philadelphia Flyers hockey game one night, and the referee tried to drop the puck in a face-off, but the puck just hovered in the air. The players and the ref stand back for a few moments, time for the paranormal puck to be caught on video from several angles. Finally the ref takes back the puck gingerly and with some hesitation he does the face-off again, and the game proceeds normally.

I ask the students to imagine how the rest of the world would react to this incident. Would there be a headline in the New York Times, "Physicists Agree Law of Gravity Invalid"? Most think not and come up with media reactions like an assumption that it was a publicity stunt rigged to increase fan attendance at Flyer games. People might think it was a holographic image of some kind.

How about suspecting that there were anti-magnets under the ice and in the puck that could be switched on remotely? What if a famous psychic had been in the audience who was known for creating psychokinetic (mind-over-matter) phenomena? Would the National Science Foundation give a large grant to a parapsychologist to study large-scale PK (psychokinesis) with this psychic? Odds against a study like this being funded by the NSF are perhaps greater than the odds against witnessing an anomalous hockey-puck drop. If the psychic's success with elevating pucks happened only rarely, would the effect be dismissed as nonreproducible? And even though the face-off had been seen by thousands, would this evidence be dismissed as "anecdotal" because it had not occurred under controlled laboratory conditions over many trials?

Another problem with using science to explore paranormal aspects of consciousness, in addition to the above, is that the subject matter appears to enter the realm of spirituality or religion, from which science has been trying to differentiate itself since the Age of Reason. John Horgan (2003: 11) reminds us that sociobiologist "Edmund O. Wilson has decreed that you cannot tread the path of spirituality and the path of reason; you must choose." For an interesting attempt to do both, see one of my favorite books: *Dialogues with Scientists and Sages* (Weber, 1986).

At this point it is time to move beyond what are mostly ideological objections to using scientific methodologies to study paranormal/spiritual topics, and to examine some more practical considerations. For example, Freeman Dyson (in Mayer, 2007: viii-ix) said that he thought that ESP exists but is scientifically untestable because it is associated with strong emotion, which is eliminated in a laboratory setting. Certainly it is a challenge to observe ESP and spirit mediumship in a lab setting without "killing the phenomenon," but it has been done rather effectively (cf. Radin, 1997 and 2006, and Schwartz, 2002), if I may editorialize.

Becker (1993: 129-138) identifies what he considers rational objections to the scientific study of the paranormal, including the problem of repeatability and the difficulty in creating an adequate theory. He also argues, however, that repeatability is not always needed or possible in science (as in some astronomical observations), and that physics sometimes can only describe, as in the case of gravity, which remains a mystery.

One of the major methodological issues we'll have to explore in greater depth later on is the use of subjective reports. Blackmore (2006: 37-38) for example discusses the problem of trying to equate reductionist studies of the brain in neuroscience to people's subjective experiences of their own consciousness. Earlier Rao (2002: 130-131) stated that most academics were skeptical about consciousness simply because they could not connect such subjective reports with neuroscientific observations.

Paul Rademacher, Director of The Monroe Institute, pointed out in his interview with me that people have known about consciousness from their own experience long before science, and that although science is useful for discovering commonalities in such experiences, there is too much of a tendency for science to become the dominant "belief of our culture."

Frederick "Skip" Atwater, who was director of research at TMI for twenty years, has great respect for scientific method, but put it in perspective for me by saying that he had done a lot of research to provide "support for what I know is obviously true." In other words, his own OBE experiences as a child were enough for him to know that OBEs exist. My favorite Skip story is about how he used to be embarrassed as a child by his bed-wetting. One night he was very certain that he had just become fully awake and had gone to the bathroom, when upon returning to bed he wet the bed again. His mother heard his outraged, frustrated cries and came running. After she had listened to Skip's complaint that he had just gone to the bathroom, his mother said, "Skip, next time you go to the bathroom, take your body with you."

Raymond Moody (1999: 113) declares that the study of near-death experiences (NDEs) has produced "very little scientific evidence; [it's] all anecdotal." Many people would think that the personal reports of NDE experiencers in Moody's famous book Life after Life (1975) were significant evidence for understanding NDEs, but Moody (1999: 7) states that the editor took out a "lengthy section at the end in which I explained in greater detail why near-death experiences can't be counted as scientific evidence of life after death."

Moody (1999: 153-154, 158-162) also points out the scientific problem of NDEs not being reproducible or replicable. And yet I thought that the whole point of Moody's using his "psychomanteum," a laboratory setting designed to generate the kind of meetings with spirit beings that occur in NDEs, was indeed to make the phenomenon somewhat reproducible (cf. Moody's *Reunions: Visionary Encounters with Departed Loved Ones*, 1993). The plot thickens.

Surely one of the basic problems with the application of scientific methodology to something as slippery as paranormal experiences is the expectation that everything amenable to science must be material or tangible, in other words a "thing" that will sit still in a test tube. Consciousness or spirit (if we dare use the word) sounds as if it might not be material; maybe it's "mind" and not "body." This gets us into "dualism", which we'll revisit later.

Interestingly the renowned linguist and activist intellectual Noam Chomsky once told John Horgan (1999, 248), "There is no such thing as the mind-body problem." Newton, he says, eliminated our last concept of a tangible "body." "Newton's own theory of gravity, which showed that objects can influence each other in nonmechanistic ways, actually shattered the materialist worldview." This means that we now realize that there can be action at a distance through immaterial properties, as in the cases of gravity, electromagnetics, and . . . consciousness. On the contrary, I should add, an inventor I talked to, in the field of electronics, told me that he disagreed with the statement by Chomsky, and said that "material" should refer to anything about which you can get information through your senses from the outside world.

Goodness. Maybe there is hope afterall for explaining apparently paranormal aspects of consciousness in a nonmaterialist way (based on Chomsky, not the inventor). By contrast again, however, one parapsychologist I interviewed couldn't think of any way to rule out other hypotheses in the alleged evidence for survival, and expected that whatever the answer turned out to be, it would all fit into normal, materialist physics.

For those who think that mainstream normal science, as an institution, is rock solid against studying the paranormal, there are nevertheless some important individual scientists who encourage it. For example, Brian Josephson, Nobel Prize winner in physics in 1973, "scolded the scientific community for refusing to consider psychic phenomena . . . [insisting that] the data are "fairly convincing"" (Horgan, 1999: 256). Josephson tried to form a psi study group at Cambridge University, where he was a tenured professor, with a mixed reaction from other physicists and from university officials.

Carter (2002: 56) discusses the tendency for scientists to be more interested in consciousness now than in the past based on two developments: the refinement of technical means for neuroscientific observation of brain activity, and increasing attempts to draw consciousness into a scientific paradigm based on quantum physics. She has also observed that some "students of neuroscience are now reading" esoteric literature and observing mystics for insights into consciousness (Carter, 2002: 277).

One more issue comes up under "What's science got to do with it?" Namely, how much are people who approach consciousness from a spiritual perspective interested in listening to what scientists have to say? When I explained my project to one Spiritualist, he said, "Let's leave the scientists out of it!" This seems like an extraordinary response from someone claiming to embrace Spiritualism (which has long claimed to be a science, a religion, and a philosophy), and I must say that this was not a typical response from the Spiritualists I have discussed this with.

As I noted earlier, The Monroe Institute is mainly interested in helping people develop their consciousness in practical ways, but they still value scientific research. Paul Rademacher told me that science is a great corrective, helping to balance an overemphasis on the subjective. He also noted that the "focus levels" they use in their consciousness exercises are science based. Patty Ray Avalon, who runs some of the programs at TMI, said that many people need science first as a way into the program, and that scientific evidence helps people in their personal evolution by verifying and explaining their experiences. Skip Atwater pointed to the importance of scientific evidence in evaluating their remote viewing experiments, and he valued quantum physics as a way to provide a theoretical framework.

OK, let's assume for sake of argument that science is a useful way of generating knowledge about consciousness. Without this assumption the book ends here. Next we need to consider how open the institution of science is to actually doing this research.

Chapter Four

WHO'S GOING TO PAY FOR THIS?

As I implied in the last chapter with my comment on the unlikelihood of the National Science Foundation (NSF) funding a paranormal hockey puck study, it is very difficult to get significant funding or other recognition for "paranormal" research from major foundations, governmental or otherwise. I think that my findings on the research activities of 91 UFO researchers (Emmons, 1997), in addition to observing what has happened when I have tried to get such funding myself, give me some good insights into how this works.

The easiest way to characterize the problem is to state that paranormal topics, like reincarnation and spirit mediumship, that fall outside the paradigms of normal science, are not likely to get funded by the scientific establishment. However, it is more complicated than that. There is a great deal of competition for grant money, and dominant groups of scientists protect their interests in the funding game by labeling other groups deviant. Thus it is in the interest of astronomers involved in SETI projects (the Search for Extraterrestrial Intelligence, based on monitoring radio signals from space) to eliminate UFO researchers from the funding game by appealing to the "flaky" image associated with the UFO topic. It is also in the interests of more mainstream astronomers to ridicule both SETI and UFO research to prevent research money from being diverted from their own work.

Fairness and logic are irrelevant in this competition. For example, I interviewed a seismologist for my UFO study (Emmons, 1997) who told me that he was heavily criticized at a seismology conference when he gave a paper that attempted to account for many UFO sightings in terms

13

of earthquake lights. One might consider this a UFO debunking talk, in that it helped eliminate an extraterrestrial intelligence explanation for some reports, but just the fact that UFO sightings (a taboo subject) was the dependent variable made the study, and the presenter, objects of ridicule at the conference.

In short, it is the subject matter that results in a stereotypic rejection of the research, almost without regard for the way the subject matter is studied. There are exceptions to this rule, and there are ways of making the study of paranormal subjects appear more legitimate. Nevertheless, in general it is in the interests of scientists who conform to the norms of mainstream, normal science, to invoke the taboo by utilizing super-skepticism to prevent research by nonconforming scientists from being funded. More on skepticism in the next chapter.

Another point worth making here is that research grant money tends to be directed toward topics that will generate money and power in the capitalist system (cf. Stanley Aronowitz's *Science as Power*, 1988). Based on this perspective, one would expect that funding for paranormal research would perk up with the anticipation of practical results. I think that this is already beginning to happen, as we shall see later on.

A good example of the problem in funding mysterious topics, even if they are not necessarily "paranormal," is the case of the placebo effect. Beauregard and O'Leary (2007, 149) attribute the difficulty in finding support for studies of the placebo effect to the fact that it cannot be patented. In other words, greater knowledge of the placebo effect might have immense health benefits, but no pharmaceutical company could make a fortune from it based on exclusive patent. As Aronowitz (1988) says, big science is structured to control people and things for political and financial purposes.

One byproduct of this system is that fields and paradigms that have failed to become legitimized within the normal science power structure will be avoided even by agencies that are relatively independent or private, outside the main control system of government and business. After all, they don't want to be ridiculed for funding "flaky" projects. A good example of this is the Templeton Foundation, which is dedicated to supporting research that will narrow the gap between science and religion.

Kelly and Kelly (2008: 73-78) state that they nominated Ian Stevenson for the Templeton Prize for several years starting in 2000, but he never received it. They argue that his pioneering research on reincarnation is an ideal example of what the Templeton Foundation says that it values, making discoveries about spiritual realities. Although the Templeton Foundation advocates bringing science and religion closer together, Kelly and Kelly (2008: 78-79) think that it takes a "thin" path of reconciliation, attempting to avoid conflict with mainstream materialist science. As I put it earlier, such an organization might be afraid of losing status or legitimacy, being very careful to avoid support of projects deemed by some not to be acceptable to science (or perhaps to some versions of religion).

Kelly and Kelly argue (2008: 79) that Stevenson was very careful to avoid injecting his own beliefs or even framing reincarnation in a spiritual way. Apparently it didn't matter. K.L. White (2008: 16), Ian Stevenson's brother, said that Ian was "shunned by most of his academic colleagues." I have a first-hand communication from one of those colleagues in the Medical School at the University of Virginia, in which Stevenson was a faculty member. The colleague told me that they did indeed consider his work inappropriate. Ironically I also saw Ian Stevenson at a meeting of the Society for Scientific Exploration, at which another member said that he tried to introduce Ian to another researcher in the field of reincarnation, but Ian declined to talk with him because he didn't think that the other man's methodology was scientific enough. All of this attempted conformity to science was insufficient, I should think because of the subject matter itself.

On a minor level, I also had an experience with the Templeton Foundation. In a preliminary discussion with a member of the organization I was told that the Templeton Foundation would never fund a study having anything to do with parapsychology . . . period. It didn't matter that my study (this one) would use a sociological frame to find out what scientists, including but not exclusively parapsychologists, thought about whether there was evidence for life after death.

In a grant-making committee at another institution, at least one member asked whether I was studying how scientists looked at life after death, or trying to study life after death itself. I replied that it would be fascinating if I could study life after death, but that that wasn't my proposal. Ironically parapsychologists are generally uncomfortable with "life after death" or anything that sounds too religious, but as in the case of Ian Stevenson, that doesn't necessarily save them from a deviant label in science. And the taint partly rubs off on me, if I dare to study them (the parapsychologists).

I apparently ran into a similar reaction among NSF reviewers in the early 2000s when I submitted a proposal for studying the New Age movement. The very subject matter seemed to be devalued. This suspicion is supported in a personal communication with an anthropologist who told me that his work in the same area was devalued simply because the subject was taboo, independent of his own very neutral approach to it.

Now for the good news. There are some sources outside the scientific establishment, especially wealthy individuals who spend their money according to their own interests and not necessarily in conformity to normal science. Ian Stevenson was supported when "Chester Carlson, inventor of Xerox, funded Ian's research and endowed his chair at the University of Virginia" (White, 2008: 16). Carlson's 1968 grant brought millions to UVA for "research on the question of survival of consciousness after death" (Roach, 2005: 269), making the University of Virginia one of three American universities with a parapsychological research unit or lab. This unit, known today as the Division of Perceptual Studies (note the legitimate sounding name), houses many scientific studies of consciousness after the death of Ian Stevenson (1918-2007).

There are other success stories as well, even involving closer involvement with mainstream science. One thing that seems to help is having advanced degrees in mainstream fields such as physics, psychology, and philosophy (rather than, for example, a PhD in parapsychology). Becoming well established with tenure at a university, and having other publications in mainstream topics help also. For example Stephen Braude, PhD in philosophy, told me he received an NIH grant for his first book and built up "deviancy credits" by becoming known in the philosophy of science before putting more emphasis into his research on psychic phenomena.

Russell Targ, a physicist, told me that he has had no problem in getting funding or in getting published in prestigious journals. Part of this is due to the fact that he was a pioneer in the development of the laser. Another reason for his success is that his research at the Stanford Research Institute (SRI), using ESP (remote viewing) to spy on the Soviet Union, was funded in the multimillions because it was useful to the CIA.

Another field in which studies of the paranormal are becoming to be recognized as relevant is medicine. Dean Radin, PhD in psychology, also trained as an engineer, is Laboratory Director at the Institute of Noetic Sciences (IONS). He told me in an interview that he is increasingly publishing in medical journals rather than in parapsychology. Along the same lines Mayer (2007: 161) points out, "It's the rare university medical center that doesn't host some study related to prayer or distant mental intention. That's a big change."

In my study of the New Spirituality (New Age) movement, I came to think that breakthroughs in the acceptance of acupuncture, meditation, and yoga demonstrate a pattern. Previously unaccepted practices in nonWestern science or in paranormal/spiritual areas are becoming legitimated mainly through medicine because of the demonstrable health (and therefore also financial) benefits in a capitalist society. Capitalism will accept the "paranormal" when it makes money.

My interviews for this study also indicate that some researchers legitimate their studies of the paranormal by framing them in ways that show their relevance to applied social and psychological programs. Some graduate students have gotten funding in this way from governmental sources in the UK. I hasten to add that the students I interviewed about these projects were genuinely interested in discovering how experiences in paranormal consciousness, such as spirit mediumship, are framed by social interaction and communication, and in making connections between the psychology of these experiences and the legitimated field of neuroscience.

One last comment about the practicality of research on paranormal consciousness and survival. Mark Nesbitt, historian, paranormal investigator, and author of popular books on the *Ghosts of Gettysburg* (1991 etc.), told me in an interview that we have spent many millions of dollars on the exploration of outer space but very little on the exploration of inner space or the afterlife. Very few of us are ever going to outer space, but the afterlife . . . we're all going there.

PART TWO

HOW WE THINK WE KNOW
WHAT WE THINK WE KNOW

Chapter Five

SKEPTICISM, RIDICULE, AND SMART-ASS JOURNALISM

By definition there can be no science without skepticism, if by "skepticism" we mean doubt, or a questioning attitude that generates knowledge based on evidence rather than sheer faith or belief. However, "skepticism" has acquired a negative connotation under one sense of the term, in which it refers to the rejection of knowledge claims without a fair examination of the evidence. Scientists whose claims, or even just their research proposals, have been rejected unfairly, sometimes accuse those who have rejected them of "skepticism," "superskepticism" or "debunking."

"Debunker" is another problematic word, used frequently in the UFO literature (Emmons, 1997: 73-83) to refer to scientists or journalists who reject UFO research without a fair hearing. These debunkers generally do not like being labeled as such, and they prefer instead to be called skeptics. Nevertheless, they often say that their mission (as in the case of CSICOP, Committee for Scientific Investigation of the Paranormal, more recently called CSI, Committee for Skeptical Inquiry) is to protect the public from unscientific misinformation (which would logically be the function of debunking).

One of my interviewees, Sarah Metcalf, a graduate student at the Anomalous Experiences Research Unit, University of York, England, had an interesting perspective. She said that she preferred not to think of herself as skeptical so much as open-minded, considering a multitude of opinions. Perhaps because we are both sociologists, I resonate to that idea as well. Although I certainly have my skeptical side, I think that I learn more by giving a variety of views (or frames) a sympathetic reading.

One of the dysfunctions of excessive skepticism is that it thwarts one of the essential components of the scientific method: the freedom to ask new questions that might revise our current thinking. Another way to put this is to say, "Nobody should be persecuted for a hypothesis." Any extraordinary or "flaky" hypothesis? In place of the aphorism attributed to the Scottish philosopher David Hume, "Extraordinary claims require extraordinary proof," I would rather say that any scientific claims require evidence, and such evidence (for or against) is not likely to surface if the research topic is labeled taboo from the outset (Emmons, 1997: 73).

Ian Stevenson, referred to in Chapter Four, dedicated his book *Where Reincarnation and Biology Intersect* (1997) "For Dr. Thomas Hunter a great Dean, profoundly skeptical of this research, equally defensive of the right to conduct it." It appears that the principle of academic freedom applies here, even if the dean didn't support the "need to conduct" the research.

For an example of kindly skepticism in academic writing, see David Fontana, *Psychology, Religion, and Spirituality* (2003). Fontana, founder of a transpersonal psychology section in the British Psychological Society, uses a moderate, sympathetic tone (what I call a "sympathetic reading"), acknowledging a variety of views, similar to Sarah Metcalf's orientation mentioned above.

For an overview of what he considers dishonesty in academe, including the ignoring of evidence, see Braude's preface to *The Limits of Influence* (1997). Radin (1997: 212-224) also discusses the tactics of trivializing the subject, showing prejudice, invalid criticisms, and distortions of the ESP literature or flawed descriptions of it in psychology texts.

Although I cannot give a lengthy, detailed review of the ESP literature here and of how it has been criticized, let me point out a few examples and point you to other sources. An interesting early example of superskeptical writing is Amy Tanner's *Studies in Spiritism* (1994), originally published in 1910. She began "in a spirit of doubt that inclined toward belief," but as an assistant to Dr. G. Stanley Hall "in his investigation of Spiritism" she came to think that "telepathy and spirit communication . . . are unsupported by any valid evidence" (Tanner, 1994: v-vi). It is difficult to know what to make of this book, because it is very negative, derogatory, and dismissive. I have, nevertheless, seen many more balanced critiques of Spiritualism at the turn of the century that have also uncovered numerous frauds and dubious cases. Gauld (1982) covers this early period and concentrates on the best cases, such as those of Mrs. Piper and Mrs. Leonard.

Science writer John Horgan (2003: 104) claims that psi has never been convincingly demonstrated in the laboratory (I think he should read Dean Radin, 1997, 2006, if he has not already). Interestingly he visited Michael Persinger's lab and reported on some experiments that resulted in 75% vs. an expected 20% accuracy (Horgan, 2003: 102), which nevertheless did not seem to alter his basic attitude. Then he wrote, "I don't believe in ESP, and I was surprised to learn that he [Persinger] does" (Horgan, 2003: 101-102). It appears that this is meant to be a reason to doubt Persinger's credibility as a researcher.

I would also like to object to the notion that such research is a matter of "belief"; I should think we were talking about evidence. I tell my class on the sociology of science at Gettysburg College that belief is an enemy of science. Once you believe 100% or 0% in anything, you are not likely to learn much more about it. Also, when people want to know your "beliefs," it may be a test of orthodoxy. Do you believe what our group expects you to? When I did research on UFO researchers, I noticed that what annoyed them most was journalists asking them if they "believed" in UFOs, to which they would reply that it was not a matter of belief but of whether the evidence was compelling (Emmons, 1997: 76).

One sociologist I interviewed who studies anomalous experiences thought that some evidence for ESP was good, but that he was by no means absolutely convinced yet. He also thought that we were not likely to get complete evidence. This is someone who is well read in the literature, and I am left with the interesting question of what evidence would be convincing to him. It certainly appears that evidence alone is not the sole determinant of acceptance, as we shall see in the next chapter. At any rate, I would consider this person a balanced skeptic.

Prominent physicist and mathematician Freeman Dyson, in the Foreword to Elizabeth Mayer's book *Extraordinary Knowing*, criticizes the early work of the Society for Psychical Research for being "anecdotal" (because it was based on people's personal accounts and not done in a laboratory) and calls the evidence for ESP by now to be "large enough to be statistically significant but not large enough to convince a skeptical critic"(Mayer 2007: viii). He then goes on to say that he considers ESP to be real but not scientifically testable. This seems odd to me, given that he presumably had access to the rest of the text of Mayer's book, which I turn to now.

Elizabeth Lloyd Mayer, a psychoanalyst and psychology professor at the University of California, Berkeley, wrote that she and most of her colleagues were uninformed about the history of psi research before she investigated it seriously. What she found involved shabby claims of bad methodology. J.B. Rhine and Louisa Rhine, the pioneering ESP researchers, beginning in the 1930s "took on every criticism" and fixed problems like "sensory leakage" possibilities in their protocols (Mayer, 2007: 90-91).

Rhine was surprised to find that his 1940 book *ESP After Sixty Years* (known as ESP-60) became required reading in introductory psychology classes at Harvard. However, "other forces denouncing ESP-60 as pseudoscience" soon prevailed, and "silence regarding anomalous mental capacities once again descended at annual meetings of the APA (American Psychological Association)" (Mayer, 2007: 92).

My psychology professor at Gannon College, John Fleming, told my sophomore psychology class in about 1962 the following anecdote that Rhine had told him. When Rhine had given an invited talk at some college, nobody showed up from the psychology department. However, as he was walking across the campus, one psychologist emerged from behind a tree and told him that he had read and admired his work, then popped back behind the tree again.

Mayer (2007: 92) says that most of her colleagues had been like her. "They'd heard of [Rhine's research], but dismissed it. Also like me, they thought they knew what they were dismissing . . . [but] we were all misinformed. So much for priding ourselves on judging by the evidence." Mayer (2007: 103, 121-126) discusses not only patterns of ignoring evidence, but also such things as misleading evaluations of evidence, as in the case of the $20-million CIA-funded remote viewing experiments by Targ and Puthoff from 1972-1995. In the latter case, one problem was that the CIA apparently deliberately mislead the evaluators on the efficacy of remote viewing (ESP).

Another good section of Mayer's book for those who would like to explore evaluations of the ESP or psi literature by an open-minded mainstream scholar involves her overview of the meta-analysis of ganzfeld studies (ESP tests in which the subjects' sensory input is limited by white noise in the ears and half ping-pong balls over the eyes) (Mayer, 2007: 196-199). In a large number of studies the cumulative result was 35% success vs. an expected value of 25% in picking out the target picture, with odds against this outcome being 10 billion to one for a sample of that size. Critic Ray Hyman considered psi impossible but conceded that the results were impressive. In a joint communiqué about these studies in 1986 Honorton and Hyman agreed to a list of more stringent protocols that would help such research in the future. "Over the next several years, more replications were produced at a series of independent labs, with an overall hit rate of 33.2 percent" (Mayer, 2007: 199).

Another subject potentially involving paranormal consciousness is near-death experiences (NDEs). Psychologist David Lester (2005: 89), who himself is critical of the quality of NDE research, says nonetheless that "The critics [of NDE research], on the other hand, have not produced a single study, poor or good." He goes on to discuss the problem of replicability and the need for large samples and controls (Lester, 2005: 91-94), and he does give examples of good NDE research.

Lester's treatment is a mixed bag in terms of how reasonable his skepticism is (at least he is skeptical of the skeptics). I did find it odd, and perhaps an indicator of undue skepticism, that he wrote, "If [NDEs] are evidence for life after death, they should be the same in every culture" (Lester, 2005: 96-97). Surely there can be cultural variations in how people interpret their NDEs (such as interpreting a spiritual figure as Buddha vs. Jesus) without this eliminating the usefulness of NDEs as evidence for survival.

Oddly Lester (2005: 153) says the same thing about reincarnation: "If reincarnation really occurs, there should be no cultural variation at all." For example, the frequency of reporting varies by society. Stevenson notes this in his work and makes the obvious point that in some countries there is more cultural opposition to reporting, such as in the United States, where there is less belief in reincarnation than in India for example. It would be fair, of course, to ask whether reincarnation belief in India stimulates false reports.

Lester (2005: 146) comments, "The notion of reincarnation is excellent since it provides explanations . . . about many phenomena [such as evidence in Stevenson's work about similarities between incarnations in terms of birthmarks, skills and interests]. This ability does not, however, prove the validity of reincarnation. A theory can be "good" yet false."

My response to that would be that any theory would be like this; good theories are "consistent with the evidence." They are also falsifiable with more evidence. It should also be noted that Ian Stevenson was very careful to use phrases like "cases suggestive of reincarnation," rather than insisting that he had "proven" anything. Nothing is ever "proven" forever in science, except for statements like "two and two are four" within the assumptions of the model.

Philosopher Paul Edwards (2002: 7-8) is even more dismissive of reincarnation, stating, "I have tried to show that this evidence [for reincarnation and karma] is worthless." His basic reasons for rejecting reincarnation involve bodily continuity and memory. "We have enormous evidence that the mind or consciousness cannot exist without the brain." Although Edwards does point up real issues in the literature, he is very unsympathetic to the evidence, and in the above statement he seems not to recognize the difficulty in proving a universal negative. How could anyone know for certain that consciousness cannot exist without the brain, even if the evidence that it did in particular cases was all poor? Also, one might want to look more sympathetically at the considerable evidence for anomalies provided by Stevenson and others for reincarnation and for other phenomena that suggest that consciousness might indeed exist beyond the brain.

Now for an example of skepticism in regard to ghosts. John Potts (2004: 223-228) criticizes ghosthunters for their "predisposition toward belief" and their pseudoscientific classification of ghosts among other things. "They partake of . . . speculation on the Internet [and have] the tendency to accept the wildest excesses of hearsay and fanciful theorizing as fact, simply because they are publicized on the Net" (Potts, 2004: 229). There is something to be said for this point of view, which resonates in fact with the criticism of ghosthunters that one hears from "paranormal investigators" and parapsychologists.

However, one might also say that Potts' article focuses on labeling ghosthunters as unscientific, instead of attempting a more sympathetic understanding by interviewing them about their attitudes toward scientific methods, and then observing how scientifically they actually conduct their ghost investigations in the field. One might also critique Potts' own (social) scientific methodology on the grounds that it emphasizes examining websites rather than doing field work based on ethnographic interviewing and participant observation. The latter two methods would probably result in a more respectful attitude and better understanding of the worldview of "ghosthunters."

As we move toward a consideration of ridicule and smart-ass journalism, physicist Michiu Kaku in his *Physics of the Impossible* (2008) writes rather like a journalist but is not so much ridiculing as dismissive (in my view). Kaku (2008: xvii) writes about "Class I impossibilities" that seem impossible today but do not violate known laws of physics. He says that this includes "certain forms of telepathy and psychokinesis." And yet not one of his 61 acknowledgments (as far as I can tell) is to a student of the paranormal (Kaku, 2008: xix-xxi). He dismisses J.B. Rhine based on Rhine's misinterpretation of the Clever Hans effect (with a horse who seemed to be able to count etc.) and the fact that a colleague was found cheating in the parapsychology lab (guilt by association) (Kaku, 2008: 73-74). He gives no mention of Rhine's important findings, in contrast to Mayer (2007).

In regard to Robert Jahn and his research on psychokinetic effects in the PEAR laboratory at Princeton, Kaku (2008: 92) says that "the effects are quite tiny . . . no more than a few parts per ten thousand on average. And even these meager results have been disputed by other scientists who claim that the researchers had subtle, hidden biases in their data." This is also very dismissive, selectively avoiding the statistics on the cumulative deviation over a very large number of trials. Also, just because somebody makes a claim about bias doesn't necessarily make it a valid claim.

Although I am less interested in popular journalists than in the perspectives of scientists, some of whom also do journalistic writing, here is a good example of what I mean by smart-ass journalism. Mary Roach in her book *Spook: Science Tackles the Afterlife* (2005: 85) writes, for example, "I don't know what homeopathists get up to nowadays, but back in the movement's infancy it was nutter central." I suppose that this could be valued for its humor, and she seems to be disclaiming any disrespect toward present-day homeopathists, based on her ignorance of their work it seems, but the real issue here is the use of "nutter" as a deviant label.

As J. Allen Hynek, the astronomer and pioneer in UFO studies once put it, "Ridicule is not part of the scientific method." However, ridicule is part of the social control system in normal science, and less than serious portrayals of a scholar's work on anomalies in popular media tend to add to the ridicule (Emmons, 1997: 27-40). Even the first word in Roach's title, "Spook," might make one wonder whether it made any rational sense for science to "tackle the afterlife."

I have one more example that borders on ridicule. It comes from an unlikely source, one would think. Raymond Moody, referred to in Chapter Three as a pioneer in the study of NDEs, wrote that parapsychologists

28

(which he does not claim to be) "masquerade as scientists, alleging they can prove mind-reading, prophetic abilities, or life after death by laboratory techniques or . . . by rational procedure. In fact, parapsychologists are pseudo-scientists, which means that they espouse a system of methods and assumptions they erroneously regard as scientific" (Moody, 1999: ix). Interestingly he doesn't like debunkers ("skeptics") either; they are really "believers in a particular ideology" (Moody, 1999: x). Nor does he like "funda-Christians." In this book (*The Last Laugh*), Moody (1999: 134-135) chooses a frame of seeing the paranormal in a playful way, connecting it to humor and entertainment.

Now let's focus on the structure of skepticism as a control system in academe. In the late nineteenth and early twentieth centuries, Harvard University psychologist William James was well aware of the scholarly rejection of psychical research in orthodox science, of the view that it was a priori impossible, and that it was being labeled as supernatural (Kelly and Kelly, 2007: xxvii-xxviii).

More recently, when Russell Targ told anthropologist Margaret Mead how disappointed he was that the scientific community would not accept ESP, "She sternly told me that I shouldn't complain because, after all, Giordano Bruno had been burned at the stake in the sixteenth century during the Inquisition for espousing ideas not very different from the ones I expressed. Bruno believed in the unity of all things, and he strongly opposed Aristotelian dualism for separating body and spirit" (Targ, 2004: 16-17).

Grossman and Hafiz (2010: 212) also parallel the rigidity of the "early renaissance Catholic Church [with] contemporary scientism . . . . So too has essential science degenerated into an equally rigid ideology of its own." Science journalist Robert Anton Wilson (1991: 20-21, 37, 45, 57), in a most amusing book, calls this The New Inquisition, a new elite scientific establishment that is not really for totally open inquiry but is based on a dogmatic "reality-tunnel," which he calls "The New Fundamentalism." Having fought the battle with dogmatic religion in the past, this scientific establishment also retains an anti-religious bias (see also Emmons, 1997: 108).

Some treatments of such ideological bias treat it in terms of world view and irrational philosophical or psychological resistance. An example of this is Michael Grosso's (2008: 549-556) discussion of "Hume's Syndrome," in reference to David Hume's rejection of evidence for healing and psychokinetic "miracles" in eighteenth-century France, because of his "fear of validating religion."

Another example of attributing resistance in normal science to individuals' adherence to dogmatic views comes from Ian Stevenson (2008: 134; reprinted from 1958), who pointed out that modern scientific knowledge differs greatly from that of the seventeenth century, "Yet we frequently overlook this and identify science with current knowledge. Those who forget that science is fundamentally a method and not a collection of facts will righteously challenge new concepts which seem to question old facts."

Without discounting the importance of the ideological positions of individual scientists who conform to normal, mainstream science, let us add to this the point that normal science is an interest group that protects its hegemonic (dominant) position. McClenon (1984: 20-26), with reference to Thomas Kuhn (1962) as well, points out that high-status scientists are unlikely to deviate from orthodox science on which their status depends. And parapsychology's anomalous data are often seen as a challenge to the "metaphysical foundations of science" (McClenon, 1984: 195). Because the stakes are high, normal science defends itself against "pseudeoscience" with rhetorical tactics like associating parapsychology, for example, with unscientific (religious or spiritual) beliefs, labeling the evidence trivial, attacking the methodology, and accusing researchers of fraud (McClenon, 1984: 81). Of course these are all potentially legitimate reasons for critiquing research, but it becomes problematic when they are politically motivated and used unfairly.

Earlier I referred to an analysis by Mayer (2007: 229-230) of a survey of academics in which 55% in the natural sciences, 66% in social sciences (excluding psychology), and 77% in arts/humanities/education thought that ESP had already been established or was likely. Only 34% of psychologists, whose discipline is most likely to be threatened or considerably revised by theories of psi (because it deals with the brain and perception), thought this. Interestingly 34% of the psychologists in the study said that ESP was actually "impossible," in contrast to only 2% of all others in the sample thinking that it was impossible. These data are consistent with the perspective that resistance to parapsychology is based on a perceived threat to normal-science disciplines and not just on personal reasoning (I'm avoiding the term "belief," because science is not supposed to be about belief). Notice also that the lowest percentage of acceptance of ESP (55%) falls in the natural sciences, consistent with the idea that the more a discipline has to do with natural science (rather than social sciences or humanities), the greater the threat parapsychology is, because it seems not to fit normal materialist science.

Perhaps you are surprised that the percentages of acceptance are so high (55%, 66%, 77%, and even 34% in psychology, the most threatened). This is interesting, because it shows perhaps that the ideas of individual scientists are more open than one would think based on the kinds of projects that are actually supported by research funding and are found in university programs of instruction (which represent the actual power structure of academe).

The same point came up in my UFO study (Emmons, 1997: 44), in which I referred to a survey done by astronomer Peter Sturrock (1994) in 1977. According to 53% of astronomers, UFOs deserved scientific study (23% said "certainly" and 30% said "probably"), and another 27% said "possibly." I referred to more such survey data (Emmons, 1997: 44) showing a majority of scientists and engineers (61%) responding that UFOs probably or definitely exist. This is astonishing until one realizes that the problem of rigidity in science has less to do with individual scientists than it does with the institution of science. In other words, rigidity in normal science is a phenomenon that needs to be analyzed sociologically and not just psychologically.

Time out for me to vent a pet peeve. This involves the way parapsychologists are attacked for their methodology, as noted above in the passage about McClenon's *Deviant Science: The Case of Parapsychology* (1984). As I shall point out shortly below, parapsychologists do this to each other as well. Lest I be accused of devaluing research methods (which would be unscientific of me), let me hasten to say that I teach sociological research methods and the sociology of science. I am more a scientist than anything else.

No methodology is perfect, and scientists always need to refine their methods. I also use multiple methodologies in my own sociological studies. For example, in our study of spirit mediums (Emmons and Emmons, 2003) we did depth ethnographic interviews with 40 spirit mediums, observed mediums in action, did a content analysis of 80 biographies of mediums, and I even became a spirit medium in order to understand what it felt like and how people were socialized to the role. When you use multiple methods, you can triangulate, checking the information from one with results from others.

Having said that, much of the attack on parapsychology has been against its methods (Mayer, 2007). Some of the debate has been appropriate, but much of it has been so excessively focused on methods that the findings themselves have been relatively ignored (as in the case of Kaku's (2008) references to J.B. Rhine and Robert Jahn that I mentioned earlier). There is no better way to appear scientific oneself than to wow your audience with your own methodology, or to attack other researchers based on their methodology. As Neil Postman (1996) pointed out, however, obsessing about methodology can obscure the important story to be told by the study.

One can always find fault with methodology, because it can never be perfect. I choose not to give a reference here, because I do not want to wallow in the nit-picking or point fingers. I read a review recently that tore into a research team involved in studying spirit mediums; it also referred to my work in the same area. Although it made some valid points, it largely ignored the significant contribution that the research had been making.

Unfortunately many scholars play the academic game of criticizing without giving a sympathetic reading in order apparently to increase their own status within a system based on conflict. This, I think, is scientifically dysfunctional, not to mention disrespectful (not nice).

OK, back to work. Having considered the problem of rigidity in normal science, let us now explore how the anomalous research opposed by normal science can actually benefit science. Peter Sturrock (2007: 241-260) discusses the role of research on different categories of anomalies and how it can help establish whether they are compatible with standard or non-standard models of reality (instead of labeling them as normal vs. paranormal or "super-natural").

Becker (1993: 147-162) proposes "a model [for understanding] resistance and change in the sciences" involving suppression, funding procedures, the development of independent research communities, their assimilation and acceptance, and issues of whether there will be recognition of new perspectives with or without actual paradigm conversion. Such discussions harken back to the work of Thomas Kuhn (*The Structure of Scientific Revolutions*, 1962), which basically theorizes how paradigm shifts occur in science not just because of the sheer accumulation of anomalies, but due in large part to social factors.

One aspect of the assimilation process in these "independent research communities" (or deviant scientific groups) is the way they try to show their commitment to scientific standards by actually overconforming. According to McClenon (1984: 164), the resistance to parapsychology from the mainstream "has caused parapsychologists to increase their own vigilance and skepticism regarding possible methodological flaws in their research."

I was surprised during the course of my interviewing and my participant observation at the meetings of the Society for Scientific Exploration, an elite organization for studying anomalies, that one scientist I highly respected was being criticized by some other scientists I highly respected for methodological flaws in his work. What I had thought, but hadn't heard them say, was that he had actually been very meticulous about continually refining his laboratory protocols in order to eliminate such possible flaws. In short, I thought that they were focusing too much on the method and not praising him for his pioneering way of testing for the phenomenon and for his interesting and highly significant results. In short, they were doing, though in a kindler, gentler way, the same thing I just criticized superskeptics for doing a few paragraphs ago.

Another interesting finding from McClenon's (1984: 166-168) sociological study of parapsychology was that respected scientists had an easier time getting their research on ESP published than parapsychologists did, but that the respected scientists had relatively sloppy research methods (for studying ESP). Therefore, ironically, one latent function of the deviant labeling of parapsychologists is that the best research on psi (that done by the parapsychologists, who have better research methods) tends to get ignored in mainstream science. Some of these respected scientists (like Puthoff and Targ) (McClenon, 1984: 168) end up improving their methods over time.

One more impact of the attack on parapsychology has been that the field has become more proof-oriented and less process-oriented (McClenon, 1984: 185). In other words, parapsychologists' first priority is to convince the scientific establishment that psi actually exists, rather than expanding knowledge about how the process works (which they also study, but which is also more of a challenge). I should think that this is why so much of parapsychology has been confined to the laboratory since the 1930s, because controlled experiments, as I tell my methods class, provide the best proof of cause and effect. Unfortunately this also means that phenomenological or subjective studies, and research in the field, a more natural setting, have been relatively neglected. More on this later.

Gauld (1982) notes that Ian Stevenson himself had been skeptical about his own research on reincarnation, and his careful critique of research methods for studying "cases suggestive of reincarnation" actually provided his own critics with ammunition to use against him. And of course some of those critics fall within the parapsychological research community.

Some scientists who have put a toe into the anomalous waters have hesitated to take the full plunge, thus censoring themselves. Mayer (2007: 17) tells the story of Robert J. Stoller who suppressed his own paper called "Telepathic Dreams?" He had discovered that his counseling patients had been dreaming about events in his life that they couldn't have known about by normal means. Fearful of scientific taboos, he did not publish the paper while he was alive; but it came out in *JAPA* (the *Journal of the American Psychological Association*) in 2001, after his death.

Philosopher Stephen Braude (1997, preface) confesses that, in spite of his earlier work with psi, he had for a time ignored evidence for large-scale PK, such as the levitation of tables. This fits the pattern discussed by Rogo and Bayless (*Phone Calls from the Dead*, 1980) in which scholars studying the paranormal tend to stick to the "normal paranormal" (like card-guessing in a laboratory) and draw a line against studying things like alleged phone calls from the spirit world or people floating up to the ceiling. Moody (1993: 35-36) pointed out that his research on stimulating encounters with the spirit world via mirror-gazing brought forth condemning reactions, in contrast to the mild reactions to his previous research on NDEs, for which "I was never scorned by skeptical scientists and physicians."

In short, the labeling of certain topics as "weird" is not limited to mainstream normal science. It happens even within the community of scholars who dare to study anomalies, partly because they want to be let into the Science Club. And lest you think that I am claiming to be perfectly open-minded, I too have my threshold of eye-rolling, although I try hard to move it higher.

I recall a friend of mine trying to get me to listen to a tape he had recorded from a radio broadcast about how hidden messages can be recovered from playing people's speech backwards. Instead of just saying no, thanks, I wasn't interested, I could actually feel myself getting angry and judgmental about what I considered a stupid claim.

This reminds me of something my friend, psychologist and UFO researcher Leo Sprinkle, once said. When we are infants sitting at a highchair, we tend to either cram the food set before us into our mouths, or toss it onto the floor. When we become adults we have the capacity to hold food in our hands and say, "I'm not sure if I want to swallow this or not." The latter is the appropriate scientific attitude.

Chapter Six

THERE'S NOTHING LIKE AN EXPERIENCE

In the last chapter we considered the issue of doubts about the appropriateness of scientific research ranging from healthy skepticism to ridicule. You'll recall that even some (many? most?) scientists who dare to study the paranormal display at least a healthy degree of skepticism themselves. Some of this is no doubt a reaction to the attack from mainstream science. However, keep in mind that scientists in general, no matter how mainstream or anomalous their subject matter, have not only been trained in the methods of science, but have also been socialized mostly in a Western cultural context that privileges science as a way of knowing. Even the spirit mediums we studied (Emmons and Emmons, 2003) tended to be skeptical of their own work, often looking for "confirmations" that their readings were evidential instead of something they were just making up in their heads.

Therefore, it often takes some kind of dramatic personal experience for a scientist to get past a materialist mindset and to become open-minded enough and curious enough to look into the study of anomalies. My favorite account of such an experience is Elizabeth Lloyd Mayer's (2007: 2-4) adventure with her daughter's harp. The expensive, handmade harp had been stolen at a theater in Oakland, California, where she played in a concert. Having failed to find it after extensive help from police, media etc., Mayer reluctantly agreed to a friend's suggestion that she contact a dowser (a practitioner who allegedly finds things, underground or elsewhere, by means of dowsing rods etc.).

Her friend directed Mayer to the president of the American Society of Dowsers, whom she then called on the phone. From Arkansas, the dowser paused briefly, then told her that the harp was still in Oakland and asked her to send him a street map of the city. Two days after she sent the map, the dowser called her back and told her, "It's in the second house on the right on D_____ Street, just off L_____ Avenue" (Mayer, 2007: 3). Mayer located the house, then gave the address to the police, who predictably told her that "a tip" was not enough grounds to get a search warrant. Besides, they said, surely the harp had been fenced out of the area by then.

At this point Mayer put up flyers in a two-block area around the house, offering a reward for the harp. "It was a crazy idea . . . [and] I was embarrassed enough about what I was doing to tell just a couple of close friends about it"(Mayer, 2007: 3). Three days later a man called saying that the harp described on the flyer he'd seen outside his house matched exactly a harp his next-door neighbor had recently acquired. After two weeks of "a series of circuitous phone calls" it was agreed that she would meet a teenage boy in a store parking lot. Sure enough, it was her daughter's harp. "Twenty-five minutes later, as I turned into my driveway, I had the thought, This changes everything . . . . I had to face the fact that my notions of space, time, reality, and the nature of the human mind were stunningly inadequate" (Mayer, 2007: 3-4.).

After that she began to delve into the literature on anomalies and started to share experiences with her psychology colleagues and others at the University of California, Berkeley, and elsewhere. She died just after completing her book *Extraordinary Knowing: Science, Skepticism, and the Inexplicable Powers of the Human Mind* (Mayer, 2007), the source for the above account.

Fortunately we have more than just "anecdotal" evidence for scientists changing their values or interests based on personal experiences (and not just on their knowledge of research findings). In a survey of elite scientists, McClenon (1984: 162) found that "belief in ESP is more closely related to personal experience [with paranormal events] than to familiarity with the research literature on psi." In other words, it may be that research is less convincing than personal experience when it comes to "things that aren't supposed to happen" (deviant knowledge).

This does not surprise me. In my study of 91 UFO researchers (84 of whom had advanced degrees, including 76 doctorates), the most important single reason they gave for wanting to (daring to) study UFOs was thinking that they had had a UFO experience themselves (Emmons, 1997: 48-54). Altogether 48% thought they had had an experience, and another 8% thought they might have. This contrasts with polls of the general population in which only between 5% and 14% thought they had seen a UFO.

Although some of these ufologists kept their work secret, most of them had undergone risks to their careers by doing UFO research. It often takes some kind of powerful personal curiosity to be willing to buck the social control system in academe and government (not so much in business). As one of the UFO researchers told me ("Dr. X", Emmons, 1997: 52-54), after he and his wife and at least one other witness had experienced a brightly-colored low-flying ferris-wheel-shaped object that drove them off the highway, he no longer doubted that UFOs existed; he just had to find out what they were.

Lest you think that an experience always carries the day ("seeing is believing"), I should point out that I had some amusing interviews with astronomers for my UFO study in which they told me that they did not believe in ESP or other anomalies, then proceeded to relate to me their own strange experiences. On another occasion I watched a tape of a man describing his disturbing nighttime visitation involving what he interpreted as a ghost, at the end of which he stated, "And I don't even believe in ghosts."

Mayer (2007: 108, 113) relates that Hal Puthoff, on the last day of the CIA-sponsored program in remote viewing that he and Russell Targ worked on at SRI, thought to himself, "I can't be doing this. These data can't be real; it's simply not possible." But the evidence was too strong. He said, "The problem lay with my beliefs." I don't want to make too much of this psychological issue, because I still think that the main issue is social organizational (the interests of the scientific establishment and of those who benefit from it), but Puthoff's case is still interesting. It shows how being socialized to the dominant paradigm makes it difficult even for scientists who dare to do the research not to be superskeptical.

Even studying how personal experience impacts scientists' willingness to study anomalies is easier for the sociologist in me to accept when I think about my own "experience with experience." Here are a couple of examples (see also Emmons and Emmons, 2003: 93-109).

Before the age of 19 I never thought that I had experienced anything paranormal, until I took the previously mentioned psychology course from Prof. John Fleming at Gannon College. Although I was an atheist at the time and felt sure that the universe could be explained entirely by the normal laws of physics, I was astonished to hear about fascinating accounts of research on ESP and PK. Instead of taking an "it can't be; therefore it isn't" attitude, however, I thought, "It shouldn't be, but it seems to be, so I'd better check it out."

I decided to try a study of my own, one in PK (mind over matter). In the following summer I rolled 3 dice at a time for a total of over 200,000 up-faces, "trying for" a 5 on each one. The results were hits 1½ to 2 percent in excess of the expected value, with odds billions to one against this outcome for the size of the sample. Prof. Fleming consulted with J.B. Rhine on my data sheets, who said they contained typical "decline effects" etc. (very cold streaks after very hot streaks). Fleming also had my dice tested (rolled in a machine) in a lab setting without me present, and the dice appeared slightly biased against fives, meaning that the odds against my results were even greater than expected.

That hooked me for life, I think, but my first actual sociological/ anthropological study of the paranormal didn't come until about 18 years later, *Chinese Ghosts and ESP: A Study of Paranormal Beliefs and Experiences*, in which I used social science to compare ghost experiences, among other things, in Western and Eastern cultures. I found basically that apparition experiences were very much the same phenomenologically, in spite of big cultural differences in beliefs (Emmons, 1982). For example, first-hand reports of apparition experiences in both cultures almost never occurred simultaneously with physical effects, in spite of strong beliefs in Chinese culture that ghosts often attack people physically.

Although I have had many other personal experiences that added to my curiosity, probably the most significant set of them got me interested in the research on spirit mediums in the U.S. (Emmons and Emmons, 2003). Most of these experiences connect to the death of my mother in 1993 (Emmons and Emmons, 2003: 101-107). I got the impression that I was communicating with my mother after her death, at first hearing her voice in my left ear. I could chalk it up to my imagination, except that there were many evidential aspects to the communication.

For example, on many occasions it appeared that she would help me find lost objects, or warn me about little accidents that were about to happen if I didn't avoid them (like a bike u-turning right back toward me, which oddly happened twice within about two minutes, with different riders on different streets). The warning was "watch out," which I heard internally a few seconds before each bicycle event. It got to the point that it seemed to me to be unscientific not to see some significance in such unusual occurrences.

Fortunately I still retain the skepticism to consider other interpretations (like clairvoyance rather than spirit communication), a point to be elaborated on later, when we discuss "phenomenological" or "subjective" evidence for spirit mediumship. Such experiences may or may not convince anybody else, but they have been enough to stimulate me to study paranormal issues (probably at a cost to my career). I also never want to lose my skeptical side. After all, my curiosity addiction is not satisfied by "believing" (I don't believe in belief; I believe in evidence, which includes personal experience). And accepting things without adequate evidence would be like cheating myself, or cheating at solitaire.

Oh, I almost forgot. I had another interesting experience in college (1964), although I thought strongly at the time that it was probably a hoax: a table-tipping demonstration (Emmons and Emmons, 2003: 137-138). At a cast party after our final performance, four of us sat around a card table with our hands on top (no thumbs underneath, it appeared). The table rose a good foot and a half before I dropped under the table to investigate. I could discover no tricks, although I suspected two people who had whispered something to each other over the table before we started.

Stephen Braude, philosophy professor at University of Maryland (Baltimore Campus), and a prominent writer in the field of paranormal research, also had a "table-up séance" experience in graduate school. He told me that several factors made it seem genuine: it was his table, the participants were not "jokers," and it was in daylight. The memory of this experience, which he thought needed confronting, stayed with him, but he waited until he was safely tenured as a professor before becoming involved in research on such matters.

Robert Waggoner (2009: 4-7), a researcher in the field of lucid dreaming, had his own experiences with lucid dreams, precognitive dreams, and visions of his "inner advisor" by ages 11 and 12. Then he read books by Carlos Castaneda as a teenager and continued to have lucid dreams, learning to practice staying aware within such dreams, which is still a practical focus of his research today.

Russell Targ, the laser physicist and remote viewing researcher mentioned above, told me about his childhood interest in trick magic, which led to his experiencing apparently real ESP while engaging in his performance tricks. His curiosity over his personal experience led him to build an ESP teaching machine involving a 4-choice option, with the target selected by a random-number generator. People could learn from feedback, knowing what it felt like when they were successful.

By contrast some researchers have become interested in anomalies without having personal experiences first to motivate them. Other strong motivators come from reading and from social influences from friends and family (some of whom may have had their own experiences). Reasons given by UFO researchers are similar (Emmons, 1997: 51). This also parallels the reasons for spirit mediums becoming socialized into their role (Emmons and Emmons, 2003: 210-217). In other words, in spite of the socialization process and social control system in mainstream science (and religion), there are other ways for people to become socialized to "deviant" knowledge.

For example, Dean Radin (1997: 300), the psi lab researcher at IONS, writes about his curiosity stemming from reading science fiction stories, something Russell Targ did as well. Radin says that people in his family, including him, did not have paranormal experiences when he was young. He never had a conversion experience and has been hooked on the data only (Mayer, 2007: 226).

Radin did tell us at a meeting of the Society for Scientific Exploration, however, that he tends to have precognitive dreams as an adult. Once he had a dream that he would be in a car accident the following day. "Not wanting to be in a car accident," he said, he decided to take a very circuitous route to work the next day, one that he did not take ordinarily . . . . But then he was rear-ended. I couldn't help speculating on how a New Ager or Spiritualist might interpret such an experience. For example, maybe the Universe was having fun with him, Dean Radin the big psi researcher, who conducts lab tests for precognition. It raises the paradoxical questions about such things as whether the future is predetermined and whether one could change it based on prior knowledge.

Darlene Miller, Director of Programs at The Monroe Institute (TMI), told me about a blend of social influence, reading, and personal experiences in her background. Having been raised fundamentalist Christian and switching to atheism in college, she was later introduced to ideas from TMI by business associates who had attended it. This plus contact with *The Course in Miracles* material changed her perspective on things. The same associates led her to try reiki healing, with which she had a dramatic experience involving intense heat that took her pain away in ten minutes. After that she took the Gateway experience from TMI and moved to TMI the following summer.

Robin Wooffitt, head of the Anomalous Experiences Research Unit, a sociological research department at the University of York, England, had early reading influences, somewhat like Dean Radin. As a child he was interested in comics, pop novels, horror films and things generally related to the occult. These led him to the paranormal and the supernatural. Although he recalled no anomalous experiences of his own as a youth, and only some things in the past few years that "could be data," he told me that nowadays he is primarily very skeptical, having been more open to such things as a child.

Al Rauber and Garrett Husveth, two paranormal investigators in the United States, both said in a joint interview that their earliest influences came from reading. Al read a book on ghosts as a sophomore in high school, then read everything he could find on the paranormal, hauntings and ESP. Garrett said that he became interested in ghosts at age five or six, then read all that he could about parapsychology, EVP (electronic voice phenomenon), ghosts and hauntings. The two of them started working together in the late 1980s. Both of them seem more focused on investigative methodology than on any personal experiences they might have had.

Mark Nesbitt, historian and writer of the *Ghosts of Gettysburg* series (1991 etc.), told me that he had been interested in ghosts as a kid, and later as a park ranger in Gettysburg he would ask people if they had heard about ghosts on the battlefield or in the historic houses there. Of course the official position of the Park Service (and of the Visitor's Center in Gettysburg, I might add, where I spotted nary a book about ghost experiences or ghost folklore) has been to deny or ignore ghost experiences, probably out of needing to appear "respectable" I should think. However, Mark, wanting to be a writer, began to record the many experiences people reported to him. And in recent years he has had some experiences of his own.

Back to academe, let me relate the background of four graduate students in the UK who were involved in studying the paranormal when I visited in 2008. Madeleine Castro, a PhD candidate at the University of York, England, said that she was curious about the unexplained from about age twelve, and she "questioned the God thing." Activities with other youths at renewal camps and around the campfire, including shared extraordinary experiences, contributed to her curiosity about anomalous experiences, which she now studies in a sociological frame.

Sarah Metcalf, also at the U. of York, whose research involves a sociological and medical approach to spirit mediumship, was originally introduced to the subject by her best friend who was a spirit medium. Sarah also attended a Spiritualist Church "for entertainment" rather than as a regular member. She started out believing in mediumship but is now agnostic about it, nevertheless retaining a research interest.

Hannah Gilbert, another sociology grad student at U. of York, told me that she had had no anomalous experiences as a child, but she did have an interest in such things that was supported by her father, an academic psychologist. They even did some work together studying spiritual healing. Eventually she ended up doing sociological research on the subjective experiences of spirit mediums.

Another graduate student, name omitted for confidentiality, was interested from an early age due to her grandmother who practiced mediumship, astrology, and tarot-card reading. As an adult she helped run a community group that held workshops in these same subjects. Although her perspective has changed from her younger years, when she "used to believe everything," she ended up studying Internet communities involved in neopaganism and Wicca.

Before concluding this chapter on how experience spurs scientists into daring to research anomalous events, I should also point out that some people take the position that experience is actually more important than science, at least in terms of convincing people to accept the paranormal as real. Tami Simon, in the editorial introduction to *Measuring the Immeasurable: The Scientific Case for Spirituality* (2008: ix-x), states, "I am not a person who needs science or research to convince me of the benefits of spiritual practice." However, Simon continues to explain that science is useful for legitimating the use of spiritual practices in the work of medical professionals, and for refining such practices.

Paul Rademacher, director of The Monroe Institute, although supportive of the use of science at TMI, said to me that we tend to think that something is real if we can prove it by science, but experience comes first. In his case, when he had a construction accident as a young man, he had the experience of breaking through the pain and into a state of peace, in which he was surrounded by a being of light. Later, while in the ministry, he heard a clear, precise voice go off in his head, telling him of a book he must read. Through such spiritual guidance he ended up at TMI.

Previously I also referred to Skip Atwater at TMI and his OBEs as a child. Those plus his involvement with remote viewing in the military left him with little doubt about the reality of such phenomena.

Finally I am reminded again of the Spiritualist who said to me, after hearing about this research of mine, "Let's leave the scientists out of it." As you should know by now, I have no intention of doing that. However, as a (social) scientist, I am still very much interested in learning from people's subjective anomalous experiences. In the next chapter I'll talk about the issue of employing research methods for doing just that.

Chapter Seven

SUBJECTIVITY

It appears from the last chapter that personal experience is a powerful motivator for getting some scientists involved in research on the mysteries of consciousness. We would expect this from a sociology of knowledge perspective in any case: people's ideas come largely from their personal experience and social background. However, powerful personal experience is probably more critical when the research is labeled deviant, because there is a strong disincentive against engaging in such research in mainstream science.

If subjective personal experiences can motivate scientists to study anomalies, does this not suggest that such experiences might also be useful evidence for the same phenomena? Ironically, subjective experiences have dubious status as evidence in mainstream science. As I will argue later, however, subjective experiences can be treated as data and used as clues to hidden processes that are difficult to study otherwise.

What lies at the heart of the problem is the mystery of consciousness, about which we have mostly subjective knowledge. This makes many psychologists very uncomfortable. In the late 1920s "J.B. Watson . . . the founder of behaviorism in psychology, declared that there can be no such thing as consciousness" (Rao, 2002: 5). In the 1970s B.F. Skinner and other behaviorists saw consciousness as an "epiphenomenon" of the brain (it must be produced by brain physiology, even if we don't know how; it can't be something spiritual or immaterial). Skinner focused on how people's habits or responses could be influenced through conditioning, and he thought that it was useless to speculate on what was happening in the "black box" of the brain, although by now neuroscientists can tell us a lot about what is going on in there.

However, in spite of the advances of modern neuroscience, we are still left with "the hard problem," which Blackmore (2006: 3) defines as "the difficulty in understanding how physiological processes in the brain can possibly give rise to subjective experiences." For example, I know when I am seeing a red rose, and if I were hooked up to brain-monitoring equipment, some activity would register. However, a scientist looking at the brain-monitor data later on would not be able to know from it that I was looking at a red rose. Nor would the scientist, or anybody else, looking at the red rose itself, be sure that her experience of the rose was the same as mine. What is the redness experience, anyway, scientifically speaking?

A review of the literature on consciousness shows repeatedly that scientists are "stuck" on knowing how to connect objective with subjective approaches to the hard problem. "Objective" science involves a scientist studying an external thing, like (somebody else's) brain, whereas subjective experience involves internal states, like one's own consciousness (Kelly et al., 2007: 51; Blackmore, 2006: 25, 36; Radin, 1997: 270-271). Scientists can't observe other people's consciousness (although in a way psychics claim to by means of telepathy).

As Blackmore (2006: 38) says, "Right now nobody knows the answer," even though neuroscientists can correlate a person's conscious thoughts with certain kinds of brain activity. Philosophy professor David Chalmers (2007: 228) says, "When it comes to the hard problem, the standard [neuroscience] approach has nothing to say."

If this is the case, it seems problematic to assume without evidence that "there is no such thing as consciousness" (Watson's highly counterintuitive idea) or that "consciousness must be an epiphenomenon of the brain" (Skinner's perspective). Noam Chomsky and others warn against "premature . . . attempts to "reduce" the mind to . . . neurophysiology" (Kelly et al., 2007: xxii).

Alright then, in the meantime, before neuroscientists manage to locate some thing or process in the brain that equates to consciousness, how about using these subjective experiences (that we all have) with our own consciousness as evidence for the nature of consciousness? Moody (1999: 113), the NDE researcher, says, "These [first-person] experiences provide us with . . . very little scientific knowledge . . . . It is difficult, if not impossible to verify, and the data are all anecdotal."

As Fontana (2003: 5), in his book *Psychology, Religion and Spirituality*, puts it, "Inner experience [is] looked on with great suspicion by many psychologists." And of course the reason for this would be that they are operating from a strict notion of science in which "objective" scientists must observe exterior objects (but they can't in this case because they can't directly observe other people's consciousness). Ironically this means that such scientists also have to ignore their own consciousness as data.

As you can well imagine, there are those who disagree with the rejection of subjective reports. As a sociologist I disagree because I am used to studying other people's subjective experiences as data, gathered through ethnographic interviews for example. My conception of science is broader than experimental laboratory science, and I think that the dismissively used word "anecdotal" is misapplied in situations involving the analysis of a significant database of personal reports.

Grossman and Hafiz (2010: 120-121) make the "radical suggestion" that instead of asking why anyone should accept the experiences of mystics and NDEers, why not ask, "What are the grounds for doubting that mystics and NDEers are . . . really experiencing what they claim to be experiencing? After all, in normal human interactions, we need a reason to doubt what someone is telling us, not a reason to believe . . . . The NDE removes all doubt in everyone who has the experience." Although I am in some sympathy with this view, I would add that rather than depend on any one person telling the truth, it might be wise methodologically to look for patterns in the data to see if there is substantial agreement.

For example, only 1 or 2 of the 76 first-hand ghost reports I collected in Hong Kong (Emmons, 1982: 39-66) involved a physical effect (including one in which a boy claimed that some shadowy ghosts had pushed him off a railway platform and onto the tracks), which supports the usual parapsychological theory that apparitions are a nonphysical ESP experience, and contradicts the Chinese cultural expectation that ghosts commonly perform physical acts. If respondents were exaggerating or lying or even just misperceiving, more should have claimed physical effects in line with the expectations of their culture about ghosts. Therefore, I think it is reasonable to conclude that these subjective reports demonstrate that the ghost experience is ordinarily mental and not physical. Not all aspects of subjective reports are so easy to deal with of course.

Rao (2002: 6-7), like Grossman and Hafiz, suggests taking subjective psi experiences seriously as evidence for "the primacy of consciousness in our being and behavior," and thinks that such a high percentage of Americans having such experiences is evidence contrary to the materialistic conception of the universe. Biologist Francisco Varela, who died in 2001, talked with Susan Blackmore (2006: 224-232) in an interview about the need for methodologies for examining inner, subjective experience of consciousness. He studied people's Buddhist meditative experiences, including his own, in the laboratory, and wanted more communication with neuroscientists about how such experiences correlated with observable neural activity.

Stephen LaBerge, a psychophysiologist at Stanford University, looked for clues to aspects of consciousness in lucid dreaming, a state in which the dreamer is aware of ("conscious of") dreaming. "Fully lucid dreamers realize . . . that the persons they appear to be in the dream are not who they really are. No longer identifying with their egos, they are free to change them" (LaBerge, 1985: 267). He thought that lucid dreaming (LD) involved transcendental experiences in which people could find out who they really were, namely connected with a unitary consciousness (we're all one) (LaBerge, 1985: 268, 271-272). His hope for the future of LD research was that scientists would find "psychophysiological relationships" between LD and physiological processes (LaBerge, 1985: 281). In other words, this brings us back to the "hard problem," trying to find correlates between subjective consciousness and neuroscientific observations of the brain.

More recently Robert Waggoner (2009: ix-x) argues that observing people who are having LDs is a good methodology for getting at the "inner observer." Moreover, he says, monitoring people involved in such things as "interacting with deceased dream figures [in LDs]" is a way to investigate dreams and the unconscious (Waggoner, 2009: x). Since LDers can communicate during the experience by moving their eyes, "Neuroscientists could potentially investigate the relationship of brain activity to subjective experience while lucidly aware and compare it to waking and [normal] dreaming states" (Waggoner, 2009: 16). Waggoner (2009: 77-84), like LaBerge, discusses issues of alteration of the self in LDs, bringing up the paradox of how self-awareness in LD can be compatible with a concept of self-lessness (being one with all) in an expanded "consciousness."

P.M.H. Atwater (2007: 205) also discusses the significance of subjective reports in the area of NDEs, and states, similarly to Grossman and Hafiz as noted above, that "experiencers themselves believe that the subjective experience of an afterlife is truthful." At least in a sociological sense this supports the idea that subjective experience is primary (more convincing than research findings for experiencers if not for others). According to Atwater's (2007: 221) data base, 60% of NDEers report significant life changes, and 19% report radical shifts ("almost as if they had become another person").

In 2008 Adam J. Rock, Julie Beischel, and Gary E. Schwartz (2008: 179-192) published an article on the phenomenological study of the subjective experiences of spirit mediums. I read it just as I was about to give my talk on "Objective and Phenomenological Methods in Mediumship Research" at the 2008 meeting of the Society for Scientific Exploration (the video of which you can see on the website of the SSE, as well as on YouTube). Significantly the Schwartz (2002) research team has also done important work studying spirit mediums in more "objective" fashion in the laboratory. Three cheers for multiple methodologies!

I also discovered later that year during my sabbatical research interviews that sociologist Robin Wooffitt and several graduate students at the Anomalous Experiences Research Unit (AERU), University of York,

England, were engaged in phenomenological studies of spirit mediumship. This included conversational analysis (how mediums and sitters talk about the spirit reading etc.), the social process within which spirit readings happen, and people's experiences with cyberpsychics on the Internet.

As Sarah Metcalf put it, scientists who test mediums usually don't understand the social (and psychological) processes involved in mediumship. Madeleine Castro commented that the social process of talking about the reading gives meaning to the "ineffable." Hannah Gilbert emphasized the qualitative methodology of letting people tell their own stories (to the sociologist), and then coming to an interpretation of the process through grounded theory (which emerges after processing the data). These are "phenomenological" studies, investigating how people themselves experience events.

As a recent example of my own similar phenomenological research on spirit mediums, in 2009 I interviewed Laine Crosby, who calls herself an "investigative medium" because she works with the police to find missing persons for example. Laine, like many other mediums we studied previously (Emmons and Emmons, 2003), says that she generally feels different when doing spirit mediumship compared to when she is picking things up clairvoyantly (psychically, using her ESP). When she's talking with a spirit it feels like a conversation, and she feels the energy of spirits in the same room.

In addition to collecting subjective experiences of spirit mediums, about which more later in the chapter on mediumship, I should also say in terms of methodology that I engaged in "participatory science," somewhat like what Varela mentioned above when he used himself as a meditation subject. I took classes in spirit mediumship, not just to observe the process but also to become a spirit medium myself in order to be able to observe the mediumship process at first hand (subjectively). Probably most sociologists would consider this a deviant methodology (maybe more because of the subject matter in fact), on the grounds that I might lose my "objectivity" by showing too little (or no) distance from the phenomenon. I, however, claim that I gained valuable insight and was still able to retain a skeptical view, which is typical of most spirit mediums anyway!

There is one other type of phenomenon I want to mention in terms of a phenomenological approach: psychokinesis (PK). Instead of rolling dice (as I did in college), nowadays tests of PK involve trying to influence the outcomes of a random-number generator with the mind. Robert Jahn and Brenda Dunne (2008: 193-213), pioneers in PK research at the PEAR (Princeton Engineering Anomalies Research) lab, call for a "science of the subjective," showing the impact of personal factors like "intention, emotional resonance . . . [and] attitude" on PK trials. Similarly Pamela Rae Heath (2000: 53-72) looked at seventeen aspects of subjective experience reported by people who had PK experiences.

Finally, perhaps I should feel guilty about not arguing for an "objective" methodological approach to the subjects of consciousness and survival. However, I take it for granted that standard scientific approaches, especially methodologies involving controlled laboratory experiments (which provide the best evidence for cause-and-effect relationships, but also have their drawbacks), are not at issue or controversial in mainstream science. I applaud those methods as well. I just want to see the expansion of available research methods, as well as the use of multiple methodologies.

Chapter Eight

A GALLERY OF FRAMES

This is a transition chapter, following mostly a discussion of science and research methodologies, and leading into several chapters on the phenomena themselves and what they might reveal about whether there is consciousness apart from the body and/or survival of consciousness after death. In case you're wondering why I didn't just start telling ghost stories right from the beginning, the hard fact is that I am a scientist at heart (with a healthy respect for intuition and other ways of knowing). Methodology really matters (to me).

Keep in mind that my main point of view is that of a sociologist, which is ironic, because I am often critical of sociology (and other sciences, social and natural). It's a little bit like rebelling against your parents . . . and then realizing that you've grown up to be just like them. But it's more than that. I have taken sociology and the rest of science seriously, which is very subversive to normal science (which limits the questions you're allowed to ask). The real spirit of science is to ask anything about any subject, and to keep an open mind.

Another thing to remember is that the central concept of this book is the "frame." Erving Goffman (1974) is the primary reference for the use of this concept in sociology: *Frame Analysis: An Essay on the Organization of Experience*. "Frame" starts out as a social psychological concept, referring to the way individuals put their own experience into some meaningful context for interpretation, and then try to communicate this frame to other people they interact with (partly by playing "language games"). "Frame" is related to other similar sociological concepts like "definition of the situation" and "symbolic interaction," all of which help explain the way social experience and knowledge are socially constructed or negotiated.

It doesn't concern me much that sociologists have used "frame" beyond the meaning Goffman had for it (and have argued about whether these other meanings are appropriate). It is enough to appreciate the central insight we can get from the metaphor of a picture in its frame. To use one of Goffman's examples, if we see two youngsters apparently fighting, it may be important to know if what they are doing is real fighting or play fighting, and whether the two of them (not to mention their parents) are seeing what they are doing in the same frame.

Carrying the frame metaphor from the realm of personal experience to the social organization of scientific knowledge is a leap beyond Goffman's original discussion, but it is useful. Different academic disciplines, for example, can look at the same general phenomenon but frame it differently. For example, a psychologist might observe our two youngsters fighting in terms of aggressive behavior. A sociologist might look for cultural norms about fighting on the playground (gang culture perhaps). A medical professional might be poised to assess and repair the damage to their bodies.

In addition, these frames become somewhat institutionalized and normalized, making it difficult to change the frames (which are now beginning to sound like Kuhn's (1962) "paradigms"). And in spite of all the talk about the value of interdisciplinary work in undergraduate education at least, it is sometimes difficult for scientists in one field to appreciate the frames used in other fields. A major goal of this book is to point this out and to overcome it.

Now, let's set out some of the possible (mostly scientific) frames for analyzing alleged consciousness beyond the brain and survival of consciousness. Keep in mind that these can be expected to overlap, and that some will be larger-scale frames than others. Atwater (2007: 195-207) considers biology, physiology and psychology. Rao (2002: 9) mentions neurobiology, psychophysiology, neuropsychology, philosophy, physics, and theology. The latter list already shows the pattern for interdisciplinary study, as in the case of "neurobiology" and "neuropsychology" which combine biology and psychology. Kevin O'Regan, interviewed by Susan Blackmore (2006: 160-172), approached consciousness issues from his focus on the mechanism of vision within psychology, for one example of a smaller-scale frame.

I would also add sociology, anthropology, and parapsychology (which itself is multidisciplinary, although often based on psychological laboratory methods) as other scientific frames. There are also religious/ spiritual frames, which are not necessarily closely linked to the "theology" perspective mentioned above. Spiritualism is interesting for claiming at least historically to include scientific, religious and philosophical frames within it. And of course keep in mind that I have claimed to be using the "frame frame," that is, looking from above at all the frames in order to try to make some sense of the big picture (picture frame). Whether or not I should be trusted is still at issue. After all, perhaps my loyalty to my background as a sociologist, anthropologist, and Spiritualist prevents me from appreciating the other frames adequately.

If I should fail to recognize this flaw in myself, at least it does not prevent me from pointing it out in others. My review of the literature has yielded some amusing apparent lack of sympathy and/or imagination in viewing things from the "frame of the other" (this is like the sociological concept of "taking the role of the other").

I think my favorite example of failing to appreciate the "frame of the other" is a statement by Francis Crick (the DNA pioneer), "If the members of a church really believe in a life after death, why do they not conduct sound experiments to establish it?" (Crick, 1994: 258). As far as I can tell, he was not joking. It probably does not take a sociologist who studies the sociology of knowledge (somebody like me) to point out that most churches would see life after death as a matter of faith rather than as a research topic. Some spiritual/religious people would see it as a matter of experience, if they've had an NDE perhaps. And finally, Spiritualists think that they actually are providing evidence for "continuity of life beyond so-called death" through spirit mediumship, not that this would typically involve "experiments."

Previously I referred to the Templeton Foundation, which did not award its prize to Ian Stevenson who was nominated for his research on cases suggestive of reincarnation (Kelly and Kelly, 2008), and which according to my source would never fund a project involving parapsychology. This is a good example of ignoring frames even when they are apparently relevant for the task, in this case, bringing science and religion together, which the Templeton Foundation is purportedly trying to do.

A century ago psychologist William James warned scientists that if they failed to respect the beliefs (and I should say experiences) of the public, then the public would fail to respect science (Blum, 2006: 26). This is about sympathetically taking the frame of the other. This statement was made in the context of debates over Spiritualism and studies of the paranormal.

One of the investigators into psychic phenomena at the time, Nora Sidgwick, thought that it was preposterous that people reported ghosts wearing clothes (Blum, 2006: 95-95). After all, humans might have souls, but surely clothes wouldn't. How could somebody see the ghost of a pair of pants? This is a nice example of premature assumptions, not appreciating that an apparition might be some kind of psychic mental construction rather than a literal view of a supernatural object. One suspects that the purpose of such an objection is to belittle the frame rather than to learn about it or from it. It parallels the attitude, "Why should outer-space aliens want to visit us?" As if we could expect to know. Both cases also reject evidence on a priori grounds; not part of the scientific method.

We need to return to the point that rejection of other frames is part of the politics of normal science, and not just ignorance of other frames. This can be seen in the case of Ian Stevenson by the way many of the critics of his reincarnation studies would find an area of weakness (which he often acknowledged himself) and then reject the whole thing without appreciating the strengths and without taking into account responses made by Stevenson (1997: 111, 179-187) and others to improve the methodology of reincarnation studies. Then "rhetorical tactics" (McClenon, 1984: 81) or "language games" (Lyotard, 1984) can be used to attack the rejected frame rather than giving it what I like to call a "sympathetic reading."

One of the reasons for rejecting other frames is the defense of boundaries to preserve the higher status of one group over another. For example, mainstream astronomy has higher prestige than SETI (monitoring radio waves from outer space to Search for Extraterrestrial Intelligence), and SETI is higher than UFO research. Spirit mediums usually think they rank higher than psychics; psychics rank higher than fortune tellers.

Sometimes this ranking-based rejection happens within scientific groups studying anomalies as well. For example, Raymond Moody (1999: 169) wrote that NDE study groups did not want to hear about his later work on simulating certain aspects of the NDE by getting people to have mirror visions of departed spirits. "Many members concluded I had gone off the deep end." In other words, NDE researchers who interview NDEers about their spontaneous experiences after the fact rank above NDE researchers who try to perform something akin to a séance.

Nevertheless, there are also scientists who combine frames or manage to transcend the usual assumptions of their disciplinary frame. For example, Mario Beauregard, neurobiologist at the University of Montreal, calls himself a "nonmaterialist neuroscientist" (a minority), and says that he knows experientially that people do "contact a reality outside [themselves]" (Beauregard and O'Leary, 2007: ix-x). He looks for neural correlates of experiences (you'll remember that idea), and says that there is a mystical state of consciousness that people are not faking and that is too complex to be explained simplistically as the effect of a God gene in our brains. Hmm. It makes you wonder if the other (mainstream) smart people doing this research are incapable of seeing this evidence, or if this is just a matter of people wearing different glasses (frames).

Now for one last provocative comment before we haul out the evidence in PART THREE. Russell Targ (2004: 155), the laser physicist and remote viewing researcher, says, "I made the transition eight years ago from hard-edged scientist to mashed potato, a more serene, happy human being." In other words, he went on a weekend spiritual retreat and retired from working at Lockheed. Based on our interview with Russell in 2009, however, I can assure you that he is no mashed potato on his intellectual side, in spite of having lit up his spiritual side. "I have learned," he writes, "that a miracle is a shift in perception, not some kind of supernatural occurrence" (Targ, 2004: 159).

Seen from the "frame frame," he's talking about changing ones frame. It reminds me of the mystical experience a philosophy professor colleague of mine told us about. One day he pulled his bicycle over to the side of the road to take a drink of water. The sun was pouring through a field of wheat beside him in late afternoon, and the whole field glistened magically. From his mindset, whatever set it off, it felt as if he could see every individual blade of wheat and as if he were one with all of it. As Targ might put it, the professor's mystical experience was not supernatural but a shift in perceptual frame. Another passerby might have seen the wheatfield merely as a source of Wheaties.

PENELOPE'S COMMENTS:

As I participated in the interviews with scientists and others, discussed with Charlie how to lay out the book and what we would write about, read what he wrote and added just a few suggestions about the research findings, I decided he had done an excellent job. There was no need for me to add other results of our research. At the same time I could see that I personally was more interested in "knowing" that comes from "within," like a mystic, rather than from "out there" like a scientist. I also discovered that the fascinating part of these topics was how individuals frame their world-view, their perception of this world and what is real, or true, for them.

In the past dozen years when I have had access to the Internet, as well as books, documentaries, and television, I have noticed that varying frames of reference for different countries, cultures, professions, even different age groups have meant that we cannot hear or see, let alone interpret, communicate, or reach consensus on information or events. My sweet father at age 95 suggested in his wisdom that he who watched FOX network all day, and I who occasionally watch Free Speech TV, give up on discussing politics and just love each other.

As I think about frames, I would be remiss if I did not include the role of early childhood in our adult perceptions of the material and non-material world. As a child I had the love and social support of my father, sister, grandparents, and extended family of aunts and cousins. And I experienced the abuse of a mentally ill mother. I now call this "the gift of the terrible mother." I learned after a childhood NDE how to travel out of my body at night, through a tunnel of light and vibration to other dimensions where I could be cherished, learn from "masters," know nearly anything. And bring the information back into my waking world. At night (and during the day), I learned to see "spirits" of people and animals, who had "died," and to see and talk non-verbally with my spirit teacher, whom I called my "Turquoise Master."

Children always learn the rules of the house. So I learned not to talk about my world-view at home with parents who truly did not understand. And I knew that across the street, my grandmother would delight in hearing what I had learned. She was a Christian mystic and a medium, so she encouraged me by teaching meditation, playing psychic games, seeing that I had spiritual teachers who were from Eastern religions, and encouraging me to give messages and spiritual teachings to the friends and ministers who visited her home. I credit her for keeping my right brain open in this way, and also my parents for seeing that I received ballet, music and dance lessons starting at age three which encouraged left/right brain development.

In addition to the NDE, I learned at a young age to go up to a corner of a room and "be a watcher" of what was happening, rather than physically experience it. This occasionally happened until I was in my twenties whenever my emotions were too intense. After years of therapy, many spiritual teachers and *The Course in Miracles* it is no longer useful and does not happen. For a long while I have recognized the CIM principle that "all that is left of the past is its beauty." And I will add: I know from experience that my consciousness is not merely contained in my brain/body.

Moving ahead to the 1980s, after studying Yoga psychology and with Native American teachers, I observed our consciousness and became aware that when a westernized American, like myself, communicated, I could sense and see the energy (aura) of our 1st, 3rd, and 5th chakras. When Native Americans (raised in their own culture), and the few people I met who were raised in India, Africa and the Middle East communicated, their 2nd, 4th, and 6th chakras were most engaged.

From these initial views of frames I become interested in NLP (Neuro-Linguistic Programming) and took classes learning to observe our individual styles of communicating. And I began to learn to meet other people where they can understand me by perceiving and attempting to use their programs or frames.

As we have been interviewing and writing, I have often wondered why many scientists are unable or unwilling to acknowledge information from outside their scientific disciplines. Why can't people accept the non-measureable aspect of consciousness? How much could we add to human evolution if we respected and incorporated not only what our left brains tell us but also our right brain functions and our spiritual self, including the wisdom of the elders of different cultures? The places we could go!

I found part of the answer as to why we get stuck in differences when I read Steve McIntosh's book *Integral Consciousness and the Future of Evolution* (2007). The book recognizes and describes how consciousness is subjective, and held by us, but also by the culture in which we participate. The cultures of the various disciplines of science are diverse with many people coming from the modernistic consciousness that has a left-brain focus on objective truth that can be materially proven. This Modernistic Consciousness was a significant breakthrough in the time of Jefferson and Franklin from the Traditional Consciousness that prevailed when they were born. Isaac Newton, Carl Sagan, and Bill Gates are good examples of Modernistic consciousness (McIntosh, 2007: 48-54).

It appears to me that some of the scientists we interviewed primarily express a Postmodern Consciousness frame with the inclusion of right brain concepts, constructivist critique, recognition of human potential and political correctness (McIntosh, 2007: 54-61). Well-known older examples of this would be John Muir and Margaret Mead.

And then there were Russell Targ and several other scientists we met who, to me, represented Integral Consciousness (McIntosh, 2007: 73-96) and my own perception of the world. These people, including Charlie, have an appreciation of conflicting truth and dialectical evaluation, aspirations for the harmonization of science and spirituality, compassion for all world-views, and insistence on achieving results. McIntosh says humans in this stage are less than 1% of the population and control less than 1% of the wealth and political power.

This consciousness is not found just in recent scientists; Albert Einstein, Teilhard de Chardin, Abraham Maslow and Ken Wilber are other examples. I would strongly recommend reading Russell Targ's (2010) delightful *Do You See What I See?* in which he recounts his life adventures exploring science and spirituality. This type of integral consciousness represents a blending of frames that contributes to a more holistic understanding of the universe.

PART THREE

TYPES OF EVIDENCE

Chapter Nine

CONSCIOUSNESS

In the next several chapters we'll look at types of evidence for consciousness beyond the body or after death (including ESP, ghosts, spirit mediumship, etc.). All of them are generally considered paranormal because they allegedly involve consciousness outside the confines of a living brain encased in a skull.

Certainly the core issue is whether we can define and observe consciousness, and figure out its limits. Previously in PART ONE we considered whether science would or could deal with questions of consciousness, and in PART TWO we asked how that might happen.

Within PART TWO, Chapter Seven focused on the apparent but problematic need to include a subjective view of consciousness, and Chapter Eight pointed to the importance of seeing how different frames (points of view) influence our understanding of the evidence.

Having said all of that, what is consciousness anyway? Whether you agree with her interpretation or not, Susan Blackmore (2005) gives a good brief overview of this scientific puzzle in her Consciousness: A Very Short Introduction.

Defining consciousness has a lot to do with the framing issue, as we'll see. Common-sensically we would probably prefer a definition something like this: "awareness of oneself and of ones surroundings." We all know when we are conscious, so what's the big deal?

Interestingly, J.B. Watson, the founder of behavioral psychology, said in the 1920s that there can be no such thing as consciousness (Rao, 2002: 5). B.F. Skinner, another behaviorist, said in the 1970s that consciousness was an epiphenomenon of matter. In other words, it's some kind of illusion based on brain functions. All of this is a reflection of the behavioral psychological frame, namely, that all we can really observe as scientists is the external behavior of humans. What goes on inside their brains could not (until recent decades) be observed "objectively."

Nils Jacobson (1974: 216-221), a Swedish psychiatrist, wrote about 21 types of consciousness, ranging from normal daytime consciousness to cosmic consciousness ("the permanent result of a mystical experience"). Eastern meditative traditions, as well as New Age treatments in the Western world, frame consciousness in a way that includes "higher levels of consciousness" beyond the individual and certainly beyond the mainstream objective methodology of neuroscience (Rao, 2002: 106-107; Horgan, 1999: 243).

Nevertheless, psychologists have gradually eroded the behaviorist taboo against talking about consciousness for a couple of reasons (Carter, 2002: 56). One is that neuroscientists can now observe the electro-chemical activity in the brains of living, conscious humans (objective data), rather than just gathering subjective reports from people about their conscious thought processes. Another reason is that quantum physics may help put consciousness into a scientific paradigm (although this is controversial).

As Gazzaniga (2008: 278) puts it, "The question of consciousness [is] like the holy grail of neuroscience." Horgan (1999: 3) says that "Consciousness is arguably the most philosophically resonant problem posed by the mind, but it is also arguably the most intractable and impractical problem."

Things have not changed much since the 1940s in this regard, when Nobel physicist Erwin Schroedinger said that scientists haven't the vaguest idea how consciousness works (Radin, 1997: 265), and when he defined consciousness as "a singular of which the plural is unknown. There is only one thing, and that which seems to be a plurality is merely a series of different aspects of this one thing" (Targ, 2004: xxv; Schroedinger, 1945).

Schroedinger's comments are still relevant today and could be understood a couple of ways. One is that each of us knows we are conscious, but how can we know for sure that anybody or anything else has consciousness? Another, from a New Age perspective, is that we are all one consciousness.

Ironically neuroscience has yet to discover a way to dispel a nonmaterialistic view of consciousness. In this sense of the term, "materialist" means that consciousness is entirely produced by the material, physical brain, and that it of necessity ceases to exist when the brain dies. A nonmaterialist view would be that consciousness is "brain plus" as Dean Radin put it when I interviewed him in 2007. Psi phenomena like ESP and spirit mediumship suggest that consciousness is "brain plus." Again, our concept of consciousness is the central problem of this book.

Why is neuroscience "stuck" in its attempt to define and observe consciousness? Well, because it has been unable to provide definitive evidence for what Francis Crick (known for his work on DNA) calls "The Astonishing Hypothesis," namely that "You . . . are in fact no more than the behavior of a vast assembly of nerve cells and their associated molecules" (Crick, 1994: 3). And, by extension, that there is no need for a soul or anything else nonmaterial in the operation of consciousness.

The idea is that eventually neuroscience will be able to find and explain consciousness by means of observing the brain in the laboratory. In the meantime, some people claim to know that consciousness is spiritual (at least in part) based upon their subjective experiences. And some psychic/paranormal/parapsychological researchers claim to have scientific evidence for phenomena that seem impossible if consciousness is indeed contained entirely within the material brain.

For now, though, let's stick with the neuroscientific frame and see where it takes us. Actually neuroscience has made great progress in explaining brain functions. It has been able to explain a lot about "easy problems" like how the brain reacts to external stimuli, how it integrates information in cognition, how it accesses its internal states, how it focuses its attention, how it controls deliberate behavior, and the difference between sleeping and waking states (Chalmers in Velmans and Schneider, 2007: 225-227).

However, neuroscience has been stymied by the (famous) "HARD PROBLEM." Can you guess what that might be? Yes, it's the problem of subjective experience or consciousness. As David Chalmers himself (who gave a famous talk on this in 1994) says, "When it comes to the hard problem, the standard [neuroscientific] approach has nothing to say" (Chalmers, 2007). Oh my. Shades of Erwin Schroedinger a half century ago. The plot thickens.

Susan Blackmore's book Conversations on Consciousness (2006) contains fascinating interviews with nueoroscientists, psychologists, philosophers and others about "the hard problem" among other things. And in fairness, they don't all think that the hard problem, or the issue of subjectivity, is necessarily that problematic. However, Blackmore (2006: 115) does point out that Chalmers' famous 1994 conference presentation on the hard problem galvanized an international movement in consciousness studies.

As a sociologist of science, I find it amusing that such a research question requires leadership and a following. What this reveals is that normal science has been reluctant to tackle this obvious problem ever since behaviorists like Watson claimed that there was no such thing as consciousness (which is so highly counterintuitive as to be apparently ridiculous). To be more charitable, we should say that given the methodological frame of behaviorism (observing external behaviors), consciousness was bound to be unobservable and therefore, from a normal scientific perspective, was as good as nonexistent.

To sum up a bit, neuroscientists have detection devices to observe what parts of the brain "light up" when it is performing various functions. However, there is no one area of the brain that has been observed to be the seat of consciousness, or as some neuroscientists put it, they can't find the control room for the "theater of the mind." And even if they could, how could they bridge the gap between objective observation of the consciousness area or function (whatever it is) and the actual experience of this consciousness?

One good way to underline this issue is with the concept of "qualia." Qualia (as in the word "qualitative") are qualitative experiences, such as our subjective experience of the quality "red." How would you describe "redness" to somebody? You might say it's the color of an apple or of lipstick, but does that really describe what red "feels like"? And how do you know that your experience of red is exactly like somebody else's? . . . . You don't . . . . You can't . . . . Maybe it's not.

We can't even know for sure that other people are really thinking the way we do, with conscious minds like ours. How do you know that everybody isn't just part of your dream? In philosophy this is called the problem of "solipsism" (entertaining the possibility that you are all there is and that everybody and everything else is merely an illusion). In fact, most of us assume that other people exist and are basically like us. As members of society we (and I as a sociologist talking about this) have to operate on this shared assumption in order to interact and organize.

While we're at it, how do we even know that we (one at a time, that is, . . . "I"). How do I know that I have a consciousness? Well, as everybody knows (notice the irony of "everybody" here), "Cogito, ergo sum." I think, therefore I am (DesCartes). Or, "I am conscious of myself; therefore, I have a consciousness."

In like manner, this has gotten some neuroscientists and other students of consciousness wondering how we could really know that other people have consciousness. And by extension whether there could (theoretically) be "zombies" (Blackmore, 2006: 7) that appear to be humanlike externally but aren't really conscious internally. In other words, just because a being puts on a show of being conscious, does that necessarily mean that it is?

This same question applies to robots and to artificial intelligence in computers (AI) (Gazzaniga, 2008: 320, 360; Blackmore, 2006: 117). If AI were developed to the point that it could perform all forms of human thought, would that automatically mean that it were conscious? Maybe we should add, would computers know they were conscious (i.e., would they be self-aware)? We want to say no, don't we?

We still have two more neuroscience-relevant questions to ponder. One is about the function of consciousness (assuming that it exists). The other is about whether the very self it tells us about is what it seems to be. These two questions are related.

First of all, there seems to be much that is illusory about our consciousness. We like to think that our consciousness is in charge of our behavior. We think about what to do, and then we do it. Neuroscientists tell us, however, that consciousness is often "backdated" (Carter, 2002: 29, 84), meaning that other parts of our brain execute movements or behaviors before we make the apparently conscious decision to do so.

Marc Jeannerod (in Velmans and Schneider, 2007: 540-550) says that we have a lack of awareness of our automatic actions, which occur faster than conscious executive action. Consciousness he calls our "narrative self," which gives us a feeling of the continuity of self, as opposed to our "embodied self," which involves moment-to-moment, discontinuous activity and is bounded to bodily events. In other words, consciousness is a bit of an illusion (more on this subsequently).

Bruce Lipton (in Simon, 2008: 192) states that 95 to 99% of cognitive activity is subconscious. Moreover the subconscious "controls almost all decisions, actions, emotions, and behaviors." Wow.

Let me share a subjective observation that I have made over the years that seems to support this unsettling concept that we are not as much in conscious control of what we do as we think we are. I have noticed, for example, that sometimes when I am about to make a quick decision about whether to go left or right around an obstacle, I find that I have already gone one way or the other before I have consciously made up my mind which way to go. Probably this happens more often than I notice, because my conscious mind comes along and "backdates" the decision, i.e. tells myself that I really decided consciously which way to go a moment ago.

Probably most of us have had the disconcerting realization that we have been driving along, turning this way and that, while in a semi-conscious fog, and wonder how we managed without "thinking." Or did we just forget (short-term memory loss)?

This relationship between the subconscious and the conscious is quite fascinating. One way to understand this might be to call it a mind/body interaction, as in the psychoneural translation hypothesis (PTH) (Beauregard and O'Leary, 2007: 150-151). This is similar to the way

70

Candace Pert ("The Science of Emotions and Consciousness" in Simon, 2008: 15-31) talks about awareness as a function of the entire organism. Pert considers the body to be the unconscious mind and says that recall is stored in the whole body, not just in the brain. What she calls "molecules of emotion" course through the body and interconnect the whole.

As an amateur observer of myself, again, (here comes another subjective report), I have sometimes observed that my body seems to have "a mind of its own." When I was in third grade I walked two miles each way to and from school. On the way home I sometimes got the urge to go to the bathroom a few blocks from home. It could be a struggle to hold it, but hold it I did until I made it to the door, and then I really had to hurry inside. It was as if my body (independent of my brain) were saying, "Okay, I had to wait until we got home, but here we are." "I" (my conscious mind) wondered why it was so hard to wait just a few more seconds.

Some neuroscientists and others using this perspective (that the conscious mind is less in control than it appears) wonder just what the function of consciousness is then, if we can pretty much operate under automatic pilot, so to speak (Blackmore, 2006: 46-47, 210). Well, I would say, that's easy. It has an executive function somewhat like the captain of a cruise ship, who doesn't micromanage the restaurant, the casino, and the spa, but keeps an overall eye on the operation. And when the need arises, as in deciding to avoid an iceberg, sometimes the conscious mind really does initiate action (Daniel Wagner, interviewed by Blackmore, 2006: 254).

Moreover, the abovementioned "narrative self" function, in which the conscious mind gives us an illusion of continuity, seems pretty important. However, here we come to a problematic concept: "the self." Crick (the DNA guy) (1994: 266) says that the conscious brain confabulates (makes up stories about what's going on) to preserve the illusion of free will. Neuroscientists can be expected to suppose that we are hard-wired to believe we have free will (Searle interviewed by Blackmore, 2006: 204), whether we do or not. A sense of free will seems to be an important piece of our concept of self.

Here's a fun fact: split-brain patients feel no different than people whose right and left halves are still connected; that is, they have no sense of dual consciousness (Gazzaniga, 2008: 295-297). This seems to be because the left brain is the interpreter and creator of self-awareness. I wonder if the fact that the two halves of the brain are still indirectly connected via the rest of the body (called the subconscious by Pert) has something to do with this.

Susan Blackmore (2006: 160-162) is adamant that consciousness and the self are made-up stories we tell ourselves about ourselves. She is famous for developing the concept of "meme" (a kind of culturally constructed meaning unit or culture trait); and she sees consciousness or the self as a meme (a story about experience). Blackmore is convinced that "true self-fulfillment and freedom come from accepting that there is no self and no freedom" (Horgan, 2003: 119).

I find this to be a delicious paradox. It reminds me of a comment by Dean Radin (Beauregard and O'Leary, 2007, back cover) about "the strange arguments offered by some scientists who insist that their minds, and yours, are meaningless illusions." The logical conclusion would seem to be that all of human science is a meaningless illusion because it is a product of minds that reason based upon the activities of their conscious minds, which are illusions.

Oddly but happily, sociology provides an interesting frame that I would argue saves the day. We sociologists are perfectly at home with the idea that culture and even our selves are socially constructed. Humans go through a socialization process in which we acquire a "self" based on our interactions with others (the "looking-glass self" as Charles H. Cooley called it).

Sociologists see no problem with understanding the function of this self. It allows us to take on social roles and to interact in an organized fashion with others. From a conflict perspective, powerful groups attempt to control how both culture and the self-concepts of others are constructed to serve the interests of the powerful. If the self is a psychological illusion or construct, it is also a social illusion or construct. Nevertheless it is also "real" in both a psychological and social sense, however it is constructed.

Noticed that we have emerged from a discussion dominated by neuroscience and entered into another realm: sociology. Let us try on another frame as well. Within the frame of standard neuroscience it is assumed that the mind or consciousness can exist only within the skull, and that psi (psychic phenomena) therefore cannot exist.

But what if we allowed a frame in which evidence for psi is considered? Would not such evidence, if it were forthcoming, in fact be support for the idea that consciousness is not necessarily strictly a materialistic brain function (Kelly et al., 2007: 1)?

As Rao (2002: 6-7) puts it, if we take psi seriously, it is an indication of "the primacy of consciousness in our being and behavior." He also refers to the high percentage of Americans who have beliefs and experiences that are contrary to a materialistic conception of the universe. Gauld (1982: 189, 204) points out that if consciousness and memory are entirely a brain function, then survival is impossible; but the best evidence for spirit mediumship suggests that survival is possible.

Neuroscientist Roger Penrose and anesthesiologist Stuart Hameroff (neither one in the mainstream of neuroscience) both considered consciousness to be "the lowest level of reality that exists" (Blackmore, 2006: 118). This is a bit like saying that consciousness is fundamental to or prior to the material world.

It is also interestingly similar to what meditation teacher Lynda Terry told me her concept of consciousness was. She said that meditation can take her to her real consciousness, which leaves her ego self and all of the surrounding material world behind. That consciousness is the oneness of everything.

Summing up again: most of this particular chapter has focused on a neuroscientific perspective on consciousness, but we have seen other frames as well. For example, there are parapsychology, sociology, and any number of spiritual views.

One of the consequences of these different frames is an inability to see beyond them (what we sociologists and anthropologists call "ethnocentrism") and to appreciate why those who use the other frames think the way they do. Recall for example Dean Radin's comment about "the strange arguments offered by some scientists who insist that their minds, and yours, are meaningless illusions" (Beauregard and O'Leary, 2007, back cover). He was referring to neuroscientists and others who explain how consciousness and the self are illusions that emerge out of brain activity (as described above). Although I sympathize greatly with Radin's frustration, we could choose to focus on the insight that a neuroscientific methodology (frame) is likely to end up with this kind of an explanation of brain and consciousness.

Having said that, it is interesting to read psychologist Michael Gazzaniga's treatment of the subject, in which he says that "There are those who feel that the essence of consciousness cannot have a physical explanation, that it is so wondrous that it can't be explained by modules and neurons and synapses and neurotransmitters. We will soldier on without them" (Gazzaniga, 2008: 278). And soldier on he does, talking about how humans tend to operate on nonreflective beliefs, i.e. believing in things like ghosts without evidence (271-272). Nowhere does he himself even consider a parapsychological approach, for example, in which the evidence for ghost experiences is examined. In short, he is content to stay within his own frame and completely ignore other frames, even though they also claim to involve "reflective beliefs" (ones that examine evidence).

Another example of ignoring other frames can be found in the way that many neuroscientists and others, like Blackmore, who focus on the "illusion" of consciousness and self, tend to leave out the sociological frame in which a constructed self is taken for granted. Another way to put this would be to say that a "reductionist" view of the self, focusing only on brain functions, fails to see the social-psychological level of reality, in which our self concepts are the building blocks.

We should also not forget spiritual approaches to consciousness, like Lynda Terry's referred to above. Meditation is another methodology for experiencing consciousness. We could choose to say that this method of knowing is nonscientific, and from the scientific frame should be ignored. We might learn more, however, if we tried to combine and integrate frames. In fact this has been going on in some circles for decades now, as in the case of Dr. Herbert Benson's studies of meditators at Harvard (Benson and Klipper, 2000).

Most of this chapter establishes the neuroscientific perspective on consciousness, looking for it strictly in terms of brain activity. As we have seen, there is no evidence, just an assumption that consciousness resides only there, or is entirely an illusion or construct based on what is there. Beginning in the next chapter on OBEs and NDEs, it is time to start looking at alleged phenomena that might indicate that consciousness is more than what goes on inside the brain.

Chapter Ten

OBEs AND NDEs

We are now starting to look at the types of evidence that might be provided for consciousness existing beyond the confines of the human skull or after the body dies. OBEs (Out-of-Body Experiences) and NDEs (Near-Death Experiences) are apparently related, the latter being generally a special case of the former. I prefer to assume that people do have these experiences (although some people might lie about having them), and leave it as an open question what these experiences in various cases might actually mean in some objective sense.

In an OBE the experiencer perceives leaving the body and looking at it from some position outside the body, usually from above. This could happen either in a waking state or when asleep, and the OBEer may then experience traveling elsewhere. "Astral projection" is another term for the same thing, but usually with a more mystical/spiritual connotation.

NDEs are OBEs that occur at the time of being in a near-death state (or when traumatized and in a fear state), such as after a serious accident or when undergoing surgery. Classic NDEs often involve the feeling of traveling down a tunnel with a light near the end and meeting beings of light, variously interpreted as relatives and friends or spiritual/religious figures. Often the NDEer perceives being told to return to life, after which there is a feeling of personal transformation. These definitions are "ideal types," and individual cases may vary or even defy categorization.

For an excellent overview of the literature on NDEs and OBEs, see Kelly et al. (2007: 367-422). Atwater (2007) presents a wide treatment of NDE issues and gives statistics from her data base of over 3000 cases. Perhaps the best analysis of whether OBEs/NDEs provide evidence for an "external" consciousness (beyond the body) and for survival is Stephen Braude's "Chapter 8: Out-of-body Experiences" in his book Immortal Remains (2003: 245-282).

Beginning in the 1970s there has been considerable discussion and debate over the meaning of these experiences. For OBEs the prime populizer was Robert Monroe's book Journeys Out of the Body (1971), and for NDEs it was Raymond Moody's Life After Life (1975).

As with many other allegedly paranormal mental experiences, there seems to be overlap with other categories of experience. For example, LaBerge (1985: 245) sees OBEs as "misinterpreted lucid dreams" [LDs] (which we consider in Chapter Eleven). Waggoner (2009: 27-28) also looks at the possible relationship between OBEs and LDs. Is remote viewing (Chapter Twelve) sometimes related to OBEs? Some ghost or apparition experiences (Chapter Thirteen) have features of OBEs as well, e.g. in "travelling clairvoyance." At the risk of giving away too much too soon, let me suggest that the "travelling" in OBEs, NDEs, LDs, remote viewing, and apparitions may be an illusion. If we are all entangled, or connected somehow with everything at a distance, as in a quantum physics perspective, information may be available nonlocally without its having to be communicated over space and time.

Before outlining the main issues regarding OBEs and NDEs, let's think about some of the frames for interpreting such experiences. One is theological. According to Mark Fox (2003: 62) there is a "deafening silence" about NDEs in theological studies, and when it is discussed it generally falls into a debate about the nature of an afterlife. In neuroscience there is an attempt, of course, to explain NDEs in terms of the neurophysiology of the dying brain. Parapsychologists, aware of the neuroscience, try to find evidence in both OBEs and NDEs that goes beyond the brain per se either to an internal ESP function or to an external or traveling consciousness outside the brain (Braude, 2003: 245-282).

One of the general issues, then, is whether OBEs/NDEs require anything external, beyond the brain. LaBerge (1985: 245), for example, seems to think not, when he says that OBEs are typically misinterpreted lucid dreams (LDs). He also refers to a study of OBE perception in which only a few of the 100 subjects' observations corresponded to what was in the target rooms (that the subjects were supposedly travelling to out-of-body). This suggests that their realistic experiences of being "out of their bodies" were "all in their heads," as in realistic "lucid dreams." Even if they had had evidential observations, these could have been interpreted as ESP rather than the result of observations made by some kind of consciousness traveling outside the body.

This same issue as to whether consciousness actually travels outside the brain came up in a discussion of remote viewing (ESP with a distant target) in our interview with Russell Targ in 2008. He told us a remarkable case of a remote viewer giving a greatly detailed description of an office in the Soviet Union, a description that Targ was eventually able to verify on a later trip to Russia. I asked him whether he thought that the remote viewer's consciousness actually travelled to the office in some physical sense, and he was reluctant to say yes. He said instead that her "awareness" travelled there.

As I pointed out above, this may turn out to be a nonissue, if we are all "entangled" with everything, and our consciousness need not travel but just be in tune with the universe. However, in the context of the OBE/NDE debate, people want to know whether apparently traveling outside one's body is evidence for consciousness existing beyond the confines of the skull.

Similarly, what are we to make of cases in which two people seem to meet when they are having OBEs? Alan Gauld (1982: 223) in discussing such a reciprocal OBE case says, "Surely we cannot avoid supposing that something (a duplicate body?) went forth from Miss Johnson which acted as a vehicle for her consciousness." From my perspective, having studied the features of apparitions in both Western cultures and in China (Emmons, 1982), I don't see how one could rule out a shared ESP in which both "travellers" focused their attention on some mutual place and created a shared ESP vision of each other. In another type of case, sometimes called "apparitions of the living" (Gauld, 1982: 224), the person having the

OBE is seen by others in the place where the OBE seemed to be taking place from the perspective of the experiencer.

Going back to Waggoner's (2009: 59) discussion of LDs, he wonders if there is any way to prove the consciousness of dream figures. This is like the zombie issue in consciousness studies! Of course in the case of reciprocal OBEs, when the OBEers share their experiences the next day by comparing notes, this clears up the situation in a way. Each person verifies for the other the consciousness of the "extra" or other person in the mutual experience.

Of course, this still doesn't provide evidence for the external physicality of the experience. Robert Monroe, pioneer in OBE experiences and research, however, reported that once he traveled out-of-body to visit a friend and saw her in her kitchen (Russell, 2007: 60). He spoke to her, and she replied. Then he pinched her just below her rib cage. A few days later, he asked her about the encounter, which she had forgotten until he mentioned the pinch. Then she showed him two marks in exactly the place he had pinched her. If we had lots of cases like this, well documented, would that prove the existence of an external consciousness? Perhaps not, if such cases could be explained by PK (psychokinetic) action at a distance, as in long-distance healing.

Another issue in the NDE literature has to do with the fact that "near death" is not the same as death. On one level this seems like an obvious point. However, it becomes significant in two ways. First, some people use this point to doubt that any experiences perceived at the end of the tunnel can represent what exists after death, since nobody who is really dead can come back to talk about it.

Second, "near death" becomes entwined with issues of clinical death and what the brain is capable of at that stage. LaBerge (1985: 258) states that after heart failure (clinical death) the brain shows considerable activity for 30 minutes or more, and he thinks that NDEs are therefore not evidence for survival (since the NDEer is not really brain dead). Atwater (2007: 161) refers to three criteria for clinical death, including lack of activity on an EEG, lack of brain-stem response to auditory stimuli, and absence of blood flow to the brain. Patients can still have an NDE under these conditions and be revived after 5-20 minutes, but sometimes even as long as 16 hours later in the morgue.

Sticklers will point out that patients who come "back to life" in such cases still cannot be said to have really died, and therefore their consciousness cannot definitively be said to have still existed separate from a living body. On the other hand, if the brain is not really functioning during the NDE, how could it be participating in the conscious awareness of the NDEer?

The most celebrated NDE case in this regard is that of Pam Reynolds (Sabom, 1998; Braude, 2003: 274). Reynolds underwent a radical brain operation in a "standstill" state, i.e. the blood was drained from her head, and her body temperature was lowered to 60 degrees. While her heart and breathing were stopped, and she had a flat EEG, she had a highly evidential NDE in which she identified conversation in the operating room about her blood vessels etc. and was later able to draw a picture of the unusual saw-like drill used in the operation. In spite of the excitement over this case in the NDE research community, there are also debunking treatments (cf., e.g., ProfWag on the website "Skepcop Forum"; August 21, 2009) that claim, for example, that the NDE began before the "standstill" state, and that some people can still be aware under heavy sedation.

Summing up some of the reasons for considering OBE/NDE experiences to be significant, Greyson (2008: 58) says that Ian Stevenson (better known for his research on reincarnation) thought that the following aspects of such experiences were suggestive of survival: accurate OBE perceptions, exceptional mental clarity when out of body, accurate perception of events at considerable distance from the body, and encounters with dead relatives and friends (some of whom the experiencer didn't even know had died). Many of these points are debated in Braude's (2003: 245-282) overview.

Atwater (2007: 195-207) identifies two types of challenges from "scientific naysayers": biological/physiological and psychological. In the former category there is for example Blackmore's dying brain theory (Atwater, 2007: 218-219), in which several aspects of the NDE experience are said to be caused by lack of oxygen etc. In the latter category, psychological, there are such things as dissociation and visual deception. Atwater tries to refute these in a variety of ways.

Nevertheless, she also states that the basic scientific problem is that the NDE "is a subjective phenomenon that has no objective criteria for validity" (Atwater, 2007: 206). In other words we must rely upon subjective experiencer reports, even if they do contain evidential elements (e.g., knowledge of activity they couldn't have perceived normally). This brings us back to the study of consciousness and the "hard problem" (Chapter Nine) and to the issue of subjective or phenomenological methods (Chapter Seven).

If we consider experiencer reports, "Experiencers themselves believe that the subjective experience of an afterlife is truthful" (Atwater, 2007: 205). From her data base of 3000 cases Atwater (2007: 219-221) reports that 60% of NDEers experience significant life changes, including 19% with shifts so radical as to become almost a different person.

Another aspect of NDEs to be considered is the social context of what people experience as they are actually about to die. The classic study of this is Osis and Haraldsson (1977), *At the Hour of Death*. More recently there is Moody and Perry (2010), *Glimpses of Eternity*.

It is one thing to read about such things as how nurses find patients talking to invisible people near the time of dying. It is another to participate in these experiences.

PENELOPE'S EXPERIENCE WITH HER DAD:

My father Jack McNab was introduced to the concept of learning how to die when he attended my class in Lily Dale on the subject six years before he died. There we discussed The Tibetan Book of the Dead, the Dalai Lama's views on death, and other traditional perspectives on how to go to the next place. We did several exercises including gathering the gifts of this lifetime and visualizing the process of talking to our body, shutting down and letting go.

Six years later, after he had pneumonia, he found himself functioning somewhat normally but facing the prospect of needing to enter a nursing home. I asked him whether he was prepared to go through more physical rehab, or to let go and go to the next place. He chose the later. I called a hospice nurse, and she came and interviewed him, my sister and me.

After she left he asked, "Am I dying?" I answered, "No." His heart and lungs were doing pretty well for 97, but we wanted everything to be in place and to provide morphine so that he could die easily when he was ready. I asked him if there was anything else he wanted to do or anybody else he wanted to see, and he said no. Then I told him that when he was ready, perhaps he could shut down his body like the Native American elders.

Although he had dressed himself and walked with the help of a walker to lunch, after the hospice nurse left and he had visited with my sister, he climbed into bed and never got up again. The following day we thought we heard him mumbling names of people like his sister who had died. As a spirit medium the only spirit I sensed was his sister, who cracked a joke and said she'd stay with him now and on the other side. From 7:00 p.m. until 2:00 a.m., although his hearing aids were out, I told him that if he wanted to stay on earth he should stay inside his body where he couldn't hear me without hearing aids. If he wanted his consciousness to hear me, he should expand his consciousness beyond his body.

Then I coached him much as in the class we had done together, recalling for him what he had told me of his life's memories, then starting with his feet thanked all the parts of his body for their many years of service, and said they could stop now. At 2:00 a.m. his breathing became very ragged, and I called the nurse to check on him. They found that all of his bodily functions were normal once they gave him a nebulizer breathing treatment.

We started the process over again of letting go until 7:00 a.m. when my sister arrived. When Charlie and I returned at 1:00 p.m. the nurse and my sister said that he was dying, but that it could take a long time. When Charlie and I entered the room, he sat up, opened his eyes, and squeezed each of our hands. Charlie said he had to drive home to Gettysburg (from

Erie, PA) and would return the next weekend, but first he would take a nap until 3:00 p.m. Pop died exactly at 3:00 p.m.

Concluding this chapter, how do OBEs and NDEs contribute to our scientific search for evidence on consciousness apart from the body and on survival? Certainly research on these phenomena is fascinating and should continue for a number of reasons. However, I essentially agree with Braude (2003) that we do not yet have much objective evidence for consciousness apart from the body or for survival based on OBEs and NDEs. What we do have is some interesting evidential cases that suggest that at least awareness (ESP) can detect phenomena at a distance.

However, we also have some fascinating subjective reports that may provide clues both to the nature of consciousness (the hard problem) and to the nature of the afterlife (if there is one) if we are willing to consider them.

Chapter Eleven

LUCID DREAMING

In the last chapter we noticed that some researchers see similarities between OBEs and LDs (lucid dreams). This is because many OBEs occur during or close to sleep, and both OBEs and LDs involve realistic-seeming adventures in consciousness without much or any participation of the body.

Two excellent books on LDs for the nonspecialist are the classic *Lucid Dreaming: The Power of Being Awake and Aware in Your Dreams* (LaBerge, 1985), and the more recent *Lucid Dreaming: Gateway to the Inner Self* (Waggoner, 2009). LaBerge wrote as a psychophysiologist doing research at Stanford University; Waggoner is the President of the International Association for the Study of Dreams, and Coeditor of *The Lucid Dream Exchange*.

Simply defined, a lucid dream is one in which you are conscious of the fact that you are dreaming, and yet you manage to keep dreaming and not wake up. People often report that their LDs are especially realistic, and perhaps more 3D and in color than usual dreams. They sometimes say that they can make conscious choices in the dream about what to do next.

When LaBerge (1985: 72-73) first tried to publish his research on LDs in 1980, he met resistance from scientists who seemed to think that LDs were impossible, but a year later he did get an article published, and there were more positive responses. This reminds me of the behavioral psychologists in the 1920s who said that consciousness was impossible. And of course the issue is much the same: how can neuroscientists verify objectively people's subjective experiences of consciousness? More about this in a moment.

Most people have had LDs, but for most people they are also rare (LaBerge, 1985: 18). I know that I can remember probably less than five in my life. What struck me most was how realistic they were, and how I could decide to move about and explore, once just within a single building, and once over a whole section of a city. I have never been able to verify the existence of what I have experienced in my LDs, but they were great fun.

LaBerge argues for the importance of studying "inner and outer" views of consciousness and says that we need scientists who study the brain but also have their own experiences, as has he (Blackmore, 2006: 147). And for this reason both scientists and New Agers have trouble with him. This reminds me of my own work on spirit mediums (Emmons and Emmons, 2003), in which I describe becoming a medium myself, and which is often too popular for the scientists and sometimes too scientific for a popular audience.

LaBerge (1985: 1-2) describes one of his own LDs in which he walks through a fabulous castle. At one point he decides which of two passageways to take. When he wants to move from place to place, he flies. Then he meets a terrifying genie, but he overcomes his fear and confronts it, taking the genie by the hands and absorbing his energy. Then he awakes "filled with vibrant energy."

I had always thought that one controls one's dreaming in an LD, as apparently LaBerge did when he decided which passageway to take, but Waggoner (2009: 19) prefers to say that the LDer "directs the focus of intent." He notes that we have a "limited realm of . . . awareness compared to the magnificent depth and creativity of . . . the dreaming." In other words, he thinks that we're not really consciously creating and controlling much of what the dream contains. Perhaps this issue of control is parallel to the issue of how much control our conscious mind actually has in the waking state as well (Chapter Nine).

LaBerge (1985: 16) says that this dreaming is more like doing than like imagining. Sexual LDs, for example, involve physical changes just as in real sex. Having such experiences seems to be one motivation for people trying to get themselves to have LDs (cf. Waggoner, 2009: 265-281, "Tips and Techniques"). Intentionally generating one's LDs is not just a new thing. Tibetan Buddhist monks as early as the eight century A.D. used yoga to "maintain full waking consciousness during the dream state" (LaBerge, 1985: 23).

Having realistic experiences in one's dreams is not the only purpose discussed for having LDs. Both LaBerge and Waggoner value the use of LDs for exploring one's true self and the nature of consciousness. "Fully lucid dreamers realize . . . that the persons they appear to be in the dream are not who they really are. No longer identifying with their egos, they are free to change them . . . ." (LaBerge, 1985: 267).

Waggoner (2009: 77) says that after twenty years of LDs "my concept of my own "self" had been altered." He then goes on to try to get in touch with a selfless state of consciousness, but runs up against the paradox of how an individual can sense and discuss a state of selflessness. He proposes that "awareness can step apart from self, then reunite with self, and that is how you coherently report about a self-less state of consciousness. The self does not experience it; the self's awareness experiences it" (Waggoner, 2009: 84).

This reminds me of our friend Doug Burns, who would probably disagree with this on the grounds that pure consciousness is undifferentiated, but a sense of self requires dualism. As in Taoism, you can't talk about "the real Tao," because it is a kind of undifferentiated nothingness (or everythingness).

Waggoner (2009: 227-243) also thinks that LDs can be used to contact the deceased. But how would we know that the dream content was not "just a dream"? Waggoner's ideas about evidential material can essentially be critiqued in the same way that the evidence from spirit mediums in a waking state can (Chapter Fifteen). He gives the example of a woman who encounters her old pastor in an LD and passes on to his living wife a message from him that the "picture of me, it is not me." When this was told to his widow, she cried and said that the message made sense to her because she had been trying to "pull him from the picture" (Waggoner, 2009: 230).

However, as with messages from waking spirit mediums, this commonsensical view of what is evidence would not be considered by most parapsychologists as ruling out telepathy, precognition or other explanations, as we'll see in Chapter Fifteen. Waggoner also considers as evidential: content referring to objects that were connected to the deceased, precognitive warnings of financial disaster, and multiple reports of contacts with the same deceased by different LDers. The latter is similar to collective apparition cases (Chapter Thirteen).

Waggoner (2009: 242) emphasizes that long, emotional, intensely interactive conversations with the deceased in an LD are experientially convincing to the NDer. This reminds me of a case in my book *Chinese Ghosts and ESP* (Emmons, 1982: 203). A spirit medium in Hong Kong had apparently brought through a Chinese woman, a friend of mine who had died in Gettysburg. When I returned to Gettysburg, I told a mutual friend about the highly evidential reading. He was interested but rather upset by the report. During my absence he had experienced an LD in which the same deceased woman appeared before him, looking at him, then turned away and disappeared. "Shaken, he wondered if she were warning him of something. He thought he had better drive carefully the next day . . . on his trip to see his fiancée . . . . The day after that, his future father-in-law had a stroke, went into a coma, and died a week later. [He] interpreted this as the reason for the dream."

Returning to a neuroscience perspective, research has been conducted since at least 1975 on how people in an LD state can consciously communicate with scientists in the laboratory by means of eye movements (Waggoner, 2009: 8; LaBerge, 1985: 68-73). They can't move anything else because the body is typically in a state of paralysis while dreaming.

LaBerge (1985: 281) sees the future of LD research as involving looking for "psychological relationships" between LD and physiological processes. Today we would say that this is part of the strategy of looking for correlates between subjective experiences of consciousness and neuroscientific observations in the laboratory.

Waggoner (2009: 16) also supports the neuroscientific investigation relating "brain activity to subjective experiences while lucidly aware, and compar[ing] it to waking and dreaming states." Again, this also involves correlating neuroscientific observations to subjective consciousness, but it still does not explain what subjective consciousness is.

However, at least it helps to distinguish what is going on in the brain when "consciousness" is happening. Interestingly, one can be conscious, that is, aware, when asleep (which is how an LD is defined). As soon as one loses the awareness of its being a dream, the LD slips into an ordinary dream. This connects to the question of what it really means to be awake. "As ordinary dreaming is to lucid dreaming, so the ordinary waking state might be to the fully awakened state" (LaBerge, 1985: 279). Now he's getting transcendental on us, and is probably going past what we can actually know from studying LDs themselves, in my humble opinion.

Perhaps we should return to the concept of "self-awareness." One can be aware of one's surroundings (as even rabbits, for example, surely are). But unless one reflects on how oneself is aware of these surroundings, there is no self-awareness. Most concepts of human consciousness contain the idea of self-awareness. I know that I know; that's self-awareness.

But are we self-aware in our regular (non-LD) dreams? Maybe so, but if we are, we become aware of an additional thing when we are having an LD: the fact that we are dreaming instead of experiencing something "real."

Next, what happens when we wake up? We become aware that the dream was not "real" if it was a regular dream. If it was an LD, we simply become aware that we have woken up; we already knew that we we're "just dreaming."

What LaBerge, Waggoner and others (including some ancient philosophers) are suggesting is that there may be other potential awakenings, and what seems like physical reality in our "waking state" is also something of an illusion. We sociologists are saying something related to this, perhaps, when we talk about our reality and our sense of self being "socially constructed." There will be more challenges to our sense of physical reality in the next chapter on ESP and remote viewing.

PENELOPE'S COMMENTS:

What is sleeping? What is awake? When I was young I talked and sleepwalked while asleep, with no memory of it. My Dad would tell me about the occurrence the following day. When I was a teen, he said I even ate pizza with him while I was asleep, which he knew by how differently I acted and sounded and by some of my responses. One night when I was 16, he came in and talked with me, asked me questions, and, because I told him the truth about where my friends and I had gone that week, I got grounded the next weekend based on my self-report. From then on it felt not safe. I didn't trust myself to sleep, but it didn't occur to me that he had done something unfair. Charlie says I often talk to him when I am asleep, but I don't make much sense in my answers to his questions, and very soon I get cranky and tell him, "I'm asleep, so please be quiet."

When I was very young (under age 5), after an NDE, I was kept in an armless blanket sleeper with a sleep strap so I had to lie on my back and could not get out of bed (supposedly to keep me warm, not sucking my thumb and not falling off the bed). I felt confined for twelve hours. It was too boring to just lie there so I learned to leave my body and astral travel to learn things. I described this process in *Guided by Spirit* (Emmons and Emmons, 2003: 46). I also learned to lucid dream. My dreams were as clear as waking life, more fun, and more in my control.

What is sleeping and staying in one's body, and what is leaving it? The first time I intentionally "astral traveled" was after a pact I made with two friends to meet in our dreams and have a conversation. We planned to write down what we learned and compare notes. The first night it "worked"; we were in different places but each experienced the same location, memory, and conversation. The second night nothing happened that I could recall. The third night I learned some things about one of the men that I could not have known by regular channels, and it created a lack of trust and respect for him. It did the service of keeping me from going into a business relationship with him. That was the only time I tried mutual lucid dreaming.

Often I do not even recall my dreams in the morning. But when I have had a troubling or recurring dream I have often decided to explore it and set the intention before sleep to watch "the movie" all the way through and remember it. The next night, before I go to sleep again, I set an intention to learn from the dream. Sometimes when I am asleep I have changed it so that I am each person in the dream and notice what it says about me. I remember a dreamtime when the person, whom I knew well, lied to me when it would have been just as easy to tell the truth. For the rest of that week when I was awake I watched that tendency in myself to stretch truth with omissions or additions. I stopped doing that, so dreaming was effective therapy.

During a troubling period when I was contemplating a divorce I would have frightening dreams. My house was being tossed on rough seas, and I was frantically running around looking for a rudder to steer the "ship" or a centerboard so it would respond to my actions as the captain. I used lucid dreaming to re-dream the dream on other nights until I had changed the course of the "ship"(my life), and arrived at a safe harbor.

At that same time I would have scary dreams where I would trip, drop a baby from a high building and run like crazy to catch her before she hit the sidewalk. Or I would be flying through a never-ending series of rooms looking for something. Another time I was running down stairs, and my purse dropped and splattered unusual (for a purse) contents all over. In my lucid dream I would pick them up, see what each item represented and claim it or throw it out. By the fourth time I had the dream it wasn't fearful, and I felt confident. I will say it took courage to be willing to go back to those frightening dreams and walk/dream through them to peaceful resolutions.

I have not had a fearful dream in at least 15 years, but I have had a few very clear and vivid dreams. Sometimes I "stop the action" and play with different outcomes. I would guess this is an important part of knowing myself, and knowing what is meant to be done (or not done) by me. I consider lucid dreams a gift and wish I had more!

Chapter Twelve

ESP AND REMOTE VIEWING

The purpose of this chapter is to consider extrasensory perception (ESP) and remote viewing (a category of ESP) in terms of what evidence they might provide for consciousness apart from the body. We can set aside the question of survival for now, although what is called ESP among the living might actually be closely related to alleged communication with the dead.

There are several interrelated concepts connected to ESP that reflect both different types of phenomena and different understandings of how they may work. Beginning in 1882 with the founding of the Society for Psychical Research in London, there was organized scientific research into "psychic" phenomena associated with Spiritualism, such as spirit mediumship and apparitions (ghosts).

The term ESP (extrasensory perception) was coined by J.B. Rhine who was famous for testing alleged psychic phenomena in a laboratory setting at Duke University in the 1930s and beyond. Within the general category of ESP are more specific concepts, such as telepathy (mind-to-mind communication), clairvoyance (mind-to-object perception), and precognition (knowing ahead of time). Spirit mediums, who claim to be speaking to the spirits of the deceased, talk about different sensory modalities, such as clairvoyance (specifically seeing "clearly"), clairaudience (hearing), and clairsentience (feeling). Paranormal olfactory sensing is sometimes referred to jokingly as "clairsniffance."

Remote viewing is really just a more recent term for using ESP to attempt to perceive and describe distant targets, as in the CIA experiments described by Russell Targ (Targ and Katra, *Miracles of Mind*, 1998). Especially clairvoyance, but also telepathy might be involved. Nowadays parapsychologists refer to all of the above under the generic term "psi," which includes all forms of ESP but also PK (psychokinesis), which is mental influence on the physical world.

Let me hasten to say that I am not going to try to establish the "reality" of ESP here by appealing to scientific evidence in published literature. For excellent overviews of the history of psi research, see Radin (*Entangled Minds*, 2006) and Mayer (*Extraordinary Knowing*, 2007: 69-212). Both of these are good in critiquing the simplistic comments one often hears from academics that ESP research is not scientifically valid or that it is not at all accepted by academics.

Mayer discusses the treatment of paranormal research by the scientific mainstream, including what she calls shabby claims of bad methodology (Mayer, 2007: 90). Interestingly, J.B. Rhine's *ESP After Sixty Years* (1940), known as ESP-60, was actually required reading at Harvard in introductory psychology for a short time before "other forces denouncing [it] as pseudoscience" prevailed (Mayer, 2007: 92).

Mayer goes on to describe patterns of ignoring evidence on the part of critics, the evaluation of the CIA remote viewing experiments, and a meta-analysis of parapsychological research in general, as does Radin (2006), who shows that the evidence overall is impressive. This is not to say that there are not special difficulties in psi research, such as problems of replicability (some recent experiments are more replicable however), and the lack of knowledge of specific mechanisms by which it might work.

This is a good time to look back at Chapter Five, in which I talk about superskepticism as a means of social control. Balanced skepticism is healthy for science, and I make no attempt to get people to "believe" in ESP. I just claim that it is worth researching. For those who reject it out of hand, I couldn't convert them if I tried.

As it turns out, even though it is extremely difficult to get institutional funding for ESP research, individual academics are more open to it than you might think. Meyer (2007: 229-230) discusses a survey of 1,100 college professors in the U.S. that found 55% of natural scientists, 66 % of social scientists (psychologists not included), and 77% in the arts/

humanities/education "believing that ESP is either an established fact or a likely possibility." Only 34% of psychologists thought so, and 34% actually thought that ESP was impossible (in contrast to 2% of all others thinking it impossible). "Impossible" is a harsh word in science, which is always supposed to be open to unlikely possibilities. One suspects that psychology is the discipline whose paradigms are most threatened by alternative concepts of consciousness.

In Chapter Six I referred to the finding from James McClenon (1984: 162) that in his survey of elite scientists, there was a much higher correlation between whether they had had a personal paranormal experience and whether they accepted ESP than there was between their familiarity with the research on psi and whether they accepted ESP. Again, "There's nothing like an experience." Even for people whose legitimate way of knowing is academic research.

Without actually reviewing the research on psi (again, read Radin, Meyer, and Targ, among others), let me give just a brief overview of how ESP has been studied. J.B. Rhine wanted to establish laboratory protocols in order to make it easier to "prove" the existence of ESP, rather than just studying spontaneous or "real-world" cases of psychic phenomena such as spirit mediumship and apparitions; although his wife Louisa E. Rhine did continue to study spontaneous cases (cf. numerous references to her work in *Chinese Ghosts and ESP*, Emmons, 1982).

One of the prime methodologies for J.B. Rhine was card guessing. Subjects tried to guess which of five symbols (circle, square, star etc.) in a pack of 25 Zener cards would come up either before (precognition) or after they had been shuffled, and with or without another person looking at the card (telepathy vs. clairvoyance). The advantage of card guessing was that a strict probability frame could be established to determine statistical significance for a given number of trials.

One main disadvantage was that gifted subjects like the famous spirit medium Eileen Garrett found the task incredibly boring after a time. Subjects often experienced decline effects, scoring very high and then trailing off even below chance near the end (psi-missing). And of course even in a laboratory setting there are opportunities for information leaking or fraud. This is true for any lab experiment, which is the reason for creating double-blind protocols, in which neither the subject nor the experimenter knows about the target.

Studying psi in a more natural setting has its advantages too, one of which is that it is less likely to kill the phenomenon, which may be very illusive or hard to generate in an artificial environment, as in the case of ghost experiences. As we will see in Chapter Fifteen on spirit mediumship, Gary Schwartz (2002) has remarkably been able to test mediums under increasingly strict laboratory conditions without killing the phenomenon.

In the case of more recent studies of ESP in the lab, more interesting tasks than card guessing have been developed, such as trying to identify a picture that someone in another room is concentrating on, or trying to describe a distant location where a target person is located (a form of remote viewing). In addition, some trials involve passive responses by the subject, such as in measuring the precognitive galvanic skin response of the subject who is about to watch randomly selected pictures (emotional vs. nonemotional) (cf. Radin, 2006). Some of these designs have proved to be more replicable than the card guessing.

Back to the question of whether all of this research has generated anything "interesting," the word Dean Radin cautiously and appropriately used when I interviewed him. I'm a firm believer in science, which means open inquiry using appropriate rational methodologies. At some point, it makes sense to give up on research that results in nothing "interesting." However, I claim that psi research has come up with a great deal that is "interesting," "suggestive," or "significant." I think the same about UFO research (Emmons, 1997).

This is not the same thing as claiming that I definitely know what ESP (or psi in general) is or how it works. I just think that the research should be done (and funded) because it is extremely important. It's important because it challenges as incomplete the normal science view of consciousness. It suggests that mind may be more than brain-in-skull.

Do I think this because of all the literature on psi that I have read? I would say yes, but there's more. Remember the significance of personal experience. I always retain some skepticism about everything; to think otherwise would be unscientific. However, I have had some zinger (apparently) ESP experiences that make it very hard for me to think that there is no such thing. Let me share a few.

I did my research for *Chinese Ghosts and ESP* in 1979-1980 with the help of my former wife Chee Lee, who was born in China and grew up in Hong Kong. One of the reasons I decided to do the research was the remarkable ESP experiences I had with her. On one occasion we decided to try a little game, in which I would think of a 2-digit number, and she would try to guess what it was. For example, I thought about, let's say, 47; . . . her guess was . . . 47. She got my next number, and the next. One chance in a million (literally). I had to stop, I was so stunned. What I should have done is keep going in the interests of science, but I couldn't. I did try it on another occasion with so-so results.

Yet on many other occasions she did equally remarkable things. I tried projecting mentally the pictures on record-album covers, and she sat in another room drawing what came to mind. Later she had to guess which of four covers had come up first, second, etc. Not only did she get a perfect score, but her pictures were uncannily similar to the target, such as four stick figures crossing a path for the Beatles' *Abbey Road* (she also wrote "Beatles" below the drawing) (Emmons, 1982: 236).

It turns out that my wife Penelope Emmons (spirit medium and coauthor of *Guided by Spirit*, 2003) is also very tuned in to me. My favorite example happened in her former home near Erie, PA, when I was helping her with a project (she didn't actually know what I was doing at that moment). I came upstairs to look for some duct tape, but I didn't say anything. I followed her through the kitchen, waiting for her to go past the drawer in which the tape was located. However, she stopped unexpectedly, pulled the drawer out, and took the tape out and set it on the counter. I asked her, "What did you do that for?" She didn't have any idea.

If these were the only things that had ever happened to me that I understood to be (or framed as) ESP, I could chalk them up to coincidence perhaps. However, I have had a great many such experiences, and they correlate strongly with certain individuals I am close to. Probably I am more impressed by such experiences than I am by the psi research, which after all, happened to somebody else.

Of course, I am not alone. As Andrew M. Greeley (1991) has said, "The paranormal is normal." If a large plurality, at least, of Americans have had such ESP experiences, does that mean anything for science? It might, if we consider subjective (or spontaneous, Louisa E. Rhine, 1978) experiences as data (Chapter Seven).

So much for an overview of the research evidence (or of reviews of and attitudes about the evidence, since I'm not trying to convince anybody in this chapter). The important question is this: if the research on ESP and remote viewing is "interesting," then what might it suggest to us about consciousness?

First of all, it is important to consider whether ESP is natural. According to Scott Rogo (1979: 284), psi is not supernatural; it's part of human nature, neither angelic nor demonic. I'm inclined to agree, but I don't see how I could prove the point. I think that all paranormal phenomena that we can get evidence about are ultimately "normal" (just not understood by current science) and natural.

However, ESP, or psychic phenomena, seems to be linked to spirit mediumship in interesting ways (Chapter Fifteen). If ESP is essentially the active ingredient in spirit mediumship, just with dead people, then ESP can be "spiritual". Does that make it supernatural? Interestingly the early Spiritualists thought in terms of natural law that everything was natural, both on the physical plane and on the higher level of spirit, just lower and higher frequencies or "vibrations." Rogo, who is now dead, might agree.

I think that we need to assume that ESP is natural (albeit paranormal by current standards). If we don't, we may get stuck in the dualistic separation of "ghost in the machine" (DesCartes) and not ever be able to connect the neuroscience to subjective consciousness (Chapter Nine).

So far, Dean Radin would probably be with us. In my interview with him in 2007 he said that the evidence for psi suggests that consciousness is "brain plus." Psi may need a brain in order to function, but it seems to connect beyond the brain by means of "entanglement" (Radin, 2006), which is the "nonlocal connections" aspect of quantum mechanics. On the quantum level, nonlocal connections have been demonstrated, for example, in experiments in which groups of photons remained coordinated at a distance, even when information could not have passed between the beams quickly enough even at the speed of light. Perhaps such nonlocal (at a distance) interconnectedness or entanglement exists on the level of larger objects as well (such as our brains).

Quantum physics suggests a model of consciousness, and of ESP in particular, that goes beyond actual communication in the ordinary sense. Hilary Evans (2002: 226) wrote, "We may find it more productive to set aside the notion of psi, as generally conceived, and to think not of simple communication but of a meeting of minds, a process . . . which is holistic rather than partial." However, Evans still finds it necessary to ask the question of whether "we each possess a supernatural body." Much of the literature on ESP and related phenomena (such as OBEs, Chapter Ten) is hung up on this issue of whether there is anything of substance that is external to the brain in a person's consciousness.

So, the core question then is whether ESP is some kind of communication, in which information travels from point A to point B (albeit mysteriously); or "just" a sharing of information on a quantum level, based on the "fact" that everything in the universe is entangled, or "nonlocally connected."

Some of the earlier experiments on ESP would seem to rule out the former explanation (communication). For example, subjects were put in a Faraday box that shielded them from any kind of electromagnetic radiation, not to mention any other means of communication like sound through the air. Before parapsychologists gravitated toward a quantum physics explanation, they were left with looking for some "paranormal" type of perception (extrasensory perception). But the fact that ESP can happen without any apparent connection in space-time (at a distance and into the future or past, and even in a Faraday box), suggests that there may be no "perception" at all. Instead of coming through a "sixth sense," maybe the information is just always available if we can pay attention to it.

And yet, people having OBEs feel like they are traveling someplace. This also reminds me again of what Russell Targ told me in the case of the remote viewer who had described in great detail an office half way around the world in the Soviet Union (Chapter Ten). He said that her "awareness" travelled there, but he wouldn't say that her consciousness had. What does this mean exactly? Mayer (2007: 260), by the way, presents the concept that remote viewers go inside, not outside, to access information. I might add that spirit mediums have various conceptions of what directions their information comes from, including sometimes from "inside" themselves (Emmons and Emmons, 2003: 255-257).

Carl B. Becker (1993: 76) talks about the "locus of perceptual consciousness" becoming exteriorized (located beyond the brain) in the case of OBEs, apparitions etc., and he thinks that life after death might be like a continuing OBE. This has a certain elegance to it, and it seems to be a frame that supports the idea of survival of consciousness. However, if the quantum physics perspective applies, and there is really no travel or communication needed to know about objects distant in space or time, there may be no need to assume survival or even a consciousness that is physically located outside the skull.

As I reread the last paragraph, I imagine myself as some 22nd century debunker saying, "See, it turns out that all of these seemingly-genuine claims of ESP were just a normal quantum-physical phenomenon, and nothing paranormal. Now that we know how all information in the universe can be accessed nonlocally, we have no need to believe that consciousness extends beyond the brain, or that this consciousness survives death." What have I done? Well, actually it's not over yet, because we still have some other phenomena to consider, like ghosts, spirit mediumship, and reincarnation (Chapters Thirteen, Fifteen, and Sixteen). We're not done with this chapter yet either, so hold on a minute.

Rupert Sheldrake's book *The Sense of Being Stared At and Other Aspects of the Extended Mind* (2003) is an interesting presentation of the view that there actually is something "out there" about our consciousness. First of all, he does acknowledge other views by saying, "Some people . . . talk in terms of vibrations, energy flow, chi, or nonlocal quantum effects [rather than fields] that link observers to what they observe" (Sheldrake, 2003: 211).

Sheldrake, by contrast, explains apparently paranormal connections among things in terms of his concept of morphic fields, which are analogous to electromagnetic fields. "Instead of thinking of minds as confined to brains, I suggest they involve extended fields of influence that stretch out far beyond brains and bodies" (Sheldrake, 2003: x).

Indeed he explains "the sense of being stared at" (such as when people seem to know when people are staring at them from behind, for which Sheldrake has various kinds of evidence, including experimental) in terms of "extended mind", the notion that something goes out from the eye in a stare, for example, which is called "extramission" (Sheldrake, 2003: 199-208). This idea has popular support. For example, Sheldrake found that 89% of a sample of college students said that they could "feel" people's stares. This fits the concept of the "evil eye," in which a stare is conceived of as a physical projection, like a ray of light. There have also been some philosophers and psychologists who have conceived of perceptions as occurring outside the head (part of "extended mind").

As much as I respect most of Rupert Sheldrake's work, I have to say that some of this hits my "threshold of eye-rolling" (speaking of eyes), which is not to say that I know it's invalid. Being charitable to my intolerant self, perhaps I just think that a quantum physical explanation, which involves no actual physical sending of influence from place to place makes more sense to me.

However, we have not heard the last word on this. After all, what about physical effects at a distance (PK and healing, Chapter Fourteen)?

Would they not seem to support Sheldrake and others who think that consciousness actually travels physically beyond the brain? First, however, we'll look at ghosts or apparitions, to see what they might tell us about consciousness both beyond the brain and beyond the grave.

Chapter Thirteen

GHOSTS OR APPARITIONS

I think that the study of ghosts is one of the most promising areas of research for providing clues both to the survival question and to whether consciousness extends beyond the brain. However, as in the case of UFO reports, the subject of ghosts is surrounded both by a cloud of cultural elaboration and by entertainment-media distortions (I thought about saying "baloney").

For a discussion of cultural variations in the uses and interpretations of ghost experiences and themes, see Emmons (2003). Earlier, in Chinese Ghosts and ESP (Emmons, 1982), I did a thorough analysis of patterns of first-hand ghost reports in Chinese culture and showed that they were very similar to ghost reports in the U.S and the UK. This happened in spite of the fact that Chinese ghost lore, stories, and beliefs are very different from those in the West, in terms of being associated with ancestor worship and emphasizing how ghosts can physically harm or help the living.

The point that first-hand ghost experiences are similar all over the world, in spite of differences in people's cultures, fits the "experiential source theory" (McClenon, 2002: 106-107). According to this theory, paranormal experiences are primary and universal, out of which different cultural (religious) elaborations develop to explain them.

For people who take ghosts seriously, like me, it's important to point out that the unit of analysis is the ghost (or apparition) experience, not the ghost. Although it is very difficult to define what a "ghost" is, it is clear that people do have ghost experiences. Probably at least ten percent of people have had at least one (Emmons, 1982: 39), although people are often uncertain how to identify and label their experiences, especially if the apparition is only auditory.

We must hasten to stipulate that many experiences that get labeled as ghosts may in fact be waking dreams, illusions (a misinterpreted normal sense experience), hoaxes (although these are rare in my view), or other normal phenomena. Parapsychologists are not very interested in these, but they do get excited about "evidential cases." These interesting cases involve either paranormal information or collective apparitions.

For an example of the "paranormal information" type, let me tell you about an experience one of my fellow college professors had. When he was about ten years old, he woke up to see the figure of the family's maid at the foot of the bed. After a moment she disappeared. He quickly got up and told his parents what he had seen, including describing what she was wearing (not a maid's uniform), but they told him that she was not in the house. Later they found out that she had died right about the time of his apparition, and she had been wearing the green dress that he had described at the time of death. This is a "crisis case" (within 24 hours of death), rather a common type, and it involves paranormal information both in terms of responding to the unknown death and in knowing about the clothing. It is evidential, therefore, suggesting that it was more than an ordinary waking dream. But is it evidence for the survival of the maid's spirit? Hmm.

The other type of evidential case is the "collective apparition." In this case there are multiple witnesses for the same apparition (or for a series of similar apparitions within a haunting perhaps). What is even better is a partially collective apparition, in which everybody present should be having the experience, but only some do. My favorite example of the latter appears in *Chinese Ghosts and ESP* (Emmons, 1982: 7-8). Fifteen or twenty Boy Scouts in Hong Kong were marching late at night. The person reporting this said that a very old couple, lit up and wearing white robes, came by them, walking strangely. Only five or six of the scouts saw them. If the couple had been "real," surely everyone would have seen them. But the fact that several scouts did see them means that it was not just a single person's hallucination.

For our purposes in this book, one important issue is whether apparitions are strictly a mental phenomenon, or whether there is some kind of paraphysical reality or spirit present in the place. I say "paraphysical" because there is general agreement among parapsychologists that ghosts are only rarely found to be really physical (not including the physical effects in hauntings, which appear to be separate from the apparitions). I was able to confirm this finding for my Chinese first-hand reports as well (Emmons, 1982: 62-66), only 2 of 176 of which contained a physical effect, in spite of the fact that Chinese cultural expectations include ghosts killing people, seducing them, and beating them at mah jong.

As Gauld (1982: 224) puts it, one parapsychological theory of ghosts involves "hallucinations" (ones based on some kind of ESP, however, not "mere" hallucinations). By this theory we suppose that the mind creates an image that imitates sensory reality, even though there is nothing physical to be sensed. Another type of theory is "animist", by which we suppose that there is some kind of spirit or consciousness in the location that the experiencer picks up on in some fashion.

Similarly, Hilary Evans (2002: 252-252) discusses this issue by saying that one option is to suppose that there is an "extended self" made up of some material unknown in current physics that can be picked up by the normal senses (similar to the animist theory above). On the other hand, perhaps a ghost has no substance at all and exists only in the experiencer's hallucination (again, however, stimulated in some paranormal fashion).

Harking back to Chapter Twelve on ESP, this is essentially the same issue about whether someone using ESP has an "extended mind" that actually travels somewhere during, let's say, remote viewing (animistic view). Or does one just become aware of information at a distance (this is like the "hallucination")?

In the case of ESP, we saw that some parapsychologists now think of awareness at a distance as fitting into the frame of quantum physics, i.e. in terms of nonlocal connections or entanglement. By analogy, we could suppose that apparitions involve some kind of nonlocal connections with a surviving consciousness. This would mean that the "ghost" is not really in the location of the apparition but is merely "thinking at" the person or place to which she/he has had some kind of attachment when alive. Maybe ghosts are never anywhere any more, having lost their physical form that used to be connected to their consciousness.

If apparitions involve communicating with other people's consciousness, then why do ghosts have to be dead to be seen? Well, indeed they do not. One of Tyrrell's (1963: 35-45) categories of apparitions is "experimental cases," in which a living person tries to send an image of him/herself to another person in another place. I have encountered cases in which this in not necessarily deliberate. Scott Rogo (1978: 138-140) discusses such cases, including one instance in which he haunted his own house, i.e. people who were staying at his house saw him there one night (when he was staying elsewhere). I think you can see the similarity to the material in Chapters Ten and Eleven on OBEs and lucid dreams. The issue there was the same: does the person's consciousness actually travel anywhere, whatever it seems like subjectively?

Remember that the "animistic" or "extended mind" or "extended self" theory of apparitions (and ESP, as well as OBEs and LDs) is based on some kind of paraphysical concept rather than on an actual physical substance (or even field, as with Sheldrake's morphic fields, which may also be thought of as paraphysical, come to think of it). We are still probably not talking about normal physical phenomena (cf. above, in which I pointed out that only 2 of my 176 Chinese ghost cases involved a real physical effect). If this is the case, then how could there ever be a photograph of a ghost, and how could ghosts produce physical effects, such as flying plates in hauntings?

Well, the first thing to remember is that the physical effects in hauntings, as I pointed out above, seem to occur separately from the apparitions (paranormal sights, sounds, smells, etc.). But we still have some photographs, some of which have been claimed to have matched what the photographer saw with his/her eyes. Although these cases are probably rare, Rogo (1978: 21) reports a situation in which one of two photographers at Raynham Hall, Norfolkshire, England in 1936 saw a ghost on a staircase, but the other one didn't. Subsequently the ghost did show up in the photograph they had taken.

How do we interpret this case? First we might think that the apparition was not there physically because the one person couldn't see it. However, if it was not physical, why did it show up on the photograph as the photographer had seen it with the naked eye? Perhaps the image involves psychokinetic (PK) energy from either the one photographer or from the spirit. This is a good example of how evidence doesn't necessarily fit just a single theory.

Rogo (1978: 37) discusses another interesting case in which pencillings appeared on the walls at Borley Rectory (a famous case in the UK) in real time as BBC engineers watched. This makes me wonder if the spirit paintings in Lily Dale, NY, that allegedly appeared on the canvas as people watched, might not be genuine after all (frankly they had hit my threshold of eye-rolling, and I had thought that they were probably fakes). But again, this physical effect was not connected to an apparition (such as a ghost holding a pencil). Nor were the "spirit" paintings in Lily Dale accompanied by apparitions of ghosts with brushes in their hands.

Although Chapter Fourteen is about physical effects (PK, Healing), we still might as well say something about poltergeists and hauntings while we're on the subject of ghosts (as you can see, there are lots of interconnections among these phenomena). As Rogo (1978: 84-95; cf. also Roll, 1972) points out, although the term "poltergeist" can be translated literally as "noisy ghost," most parapsychologists use the term to refer to cases in which the physical effects seem to be generated by the frustrated psychic energy of a single living "focus person," typically a youngster between 11 and 17, and classically a 14-year-old girl who suppresses her anger against other members of the household.

Poltergeist effects typically include object throwing (often without breaking when it seems it should), rapping noises, spontaneous fires, and the disappearing and reappearing of objects (Rogo, 1978: 92). The same effects can occur in hauntings (thought to be caused by spirits of the dead, rather than by PK of the living), but generally the physical effects apparently due to a living poltergeist focus are more powerful than those in hauntings.

Try as we might to categorize paranormal phenomena as one thing or the other, there are interesting cases that seem to combine two or more categories. Summarizing one of my cases in *Chinese Ghosts and ESP* (Emmons, 1982: 137-138), a 19-year old woman reported, "An aunt of ours . . . had a dream that [my cousin who had just died 21 days before] came back and visited all the extended family. That same night my picture fell off the bedroom wall, and the embroidery he gave me was twisted up on the wall. I have a picture of myself on the wall [and] on another wall there's the embroidery he gave me, along with a picture of the Holy Family [which wasn't moved]."

The interviewee told me that the embroidery stayed on the hook, but the bottom was rotated up to the right side. Both the embroidery and the picture that fell had been put on with string twisted clockwise around a nail. Since neither nail had come out of the wall, we can imagine an opposite force in the room reversing the process that night.

When I asked the woman if she was the type to get angry with people when she got frustrated, she said, "No, I keep it inside," which is a personality characteristic of poltergeist focuses. As for the emotional motive in this case, her "cousin" was not genetically related but rather connected to her through adoption. He was actually her boyfriend, and the cause of death was 35 knife wounds to the head by his mentally disturbed brother.

Such a trauma might have led to a psychokinetic outburst (either from her as a living poltergeist focus, or from him the spirit, or a combination of the two) on the surrounding environment of her room. Notice that the energy was selective, affecting only items of personal interest to the two of them: her picture and his embroidery gift, but not the Holy Family picture.

Add to this the interesting cultural "fact that it occurred on the twenty-first day after death, a prime date in ancestor-worship culture [when ghosts of ancestors are expected to return, which] may have timed the release of PK according to her expectations. Perhaps the aunt's dream fit the same expectations independently. Alternately the two occurrences might have been linked by ESP between the woman and her aunt, or the spirit might actually have contacted the aunt and had a hand in the movement of the frames on the wall" (Emmons, 1982: 138).

Certainly emotion seems to be a common trigger in paranormal cases of many types, including ESP between a mother and a child she somehow knows is in danger. In the Chinese case above, the young woman's boyfriend died a violent death, caused within the family no less. It seems to fit the "failure to adjust" theory discussed in Evans (2002: 101), which can be applied both to apparitions (maybe especially to hauntings) and to reincarnation cases. As we shall see in Chapter Sixteen, people seeming to remember past lives have allegedly died from violent deaths in the previous life at a rate well beyond chance. Evans (2002: 102) considers haunting and reincarnation as alternatives, in that each may represent a spirit unable to let go of a traumatic event in the previous life (having failed to adjust to it after death).

This point also belongs in the wider discussion of what the motivation seems to be for this alleged contact between the living and the dead (which would be evidence for survival). We can imagine that someone dying a violent death would be unwilling to let go of problems in life. This turns out to be a major theme in regard to ghosts in world cultures (although this by itself is not evidence for survival).

In the Chinese case (Emmons, 1982: 20-27), ghosts who return to contact the living, either through spirit mediums or by haunting people, may have committed suicide or have been murdered, or may have had unfulfilled social lives, such as being childless or not having been buried properly. The dead and the living are thought to help each other when ancestor worship is practiced properly. I'll burn incense for you, and you (my dead relative) will make me rich.

Going back to parapsychological theory, ghosts seem to be attached either to people they knew well (as with the professor's maid), or to places important to them (as with soldiers haunting a battlefield). Of course we must be careful to consider possible motivations of the living to imagine such contacts, because they were also attached to the person who died, and they may expect battlefields to be haunted.

Especially in Chinese culture, it is common for people to be afraid of ghosts (which they take seriously), and therefore to assume violent intent in many ghosts. However, this also happens to a lesser degree in the United States. Rogo (1978: 64-69), having made an extensive review of serious studies of ghosts or apparitions, said that evil hauntings or presences are rare, but they do seem to occur.

I noticed in my study of Chinese ghosts that many experiencers expressed fear, often without the content of the experience giving any substantive evidence for evil intent on the part of the ghost. One woman did say that she thought that male ghosts were trying to attack her in the shower.

For quite a number of years I used to get phone calls from a woman in the Midwest who knew that I had studied ghosts. Several things occurred in her residence that frightened her, and which she attributed to some kind of spiritual evil. For example, it used to get unusually hot for no reason, and especially in her child's crib, which worried her a great deal. The fire department came and was perplexed. Of course I referred her to other people who might be able to help her, including religious practitioners. No matter what was actually happening, and I did not claim to know, she certainly needed to be taken seriously.

Notice that the idea of ghosts hanging around with violent or disturbed motivations implies that there is a surviving spirit with an active intent toward the living. Therefore, this view would seem to be at odds with another perspective that we have not considered yet: namely that ghosts are merely some kind of residual energy left in a place.

Gauld (1982: 248-249) refers to this as "retrocognitive [looking back into the past with ones ESP] or playback theory," which would especially be applied to hauntings (ghosts attached to a place). He recognizes that this seems to fit cases in which people see past battles, as in a case reported to me about a man who was very frightened when he witnessed what looked like Pickett's Charge happening realistically right in front of him when he was at the "High Watermark of the Confederacy" spot on the Gettysburg battlefield.

However, Gauld also recognizes that the retrocognitive theory doesn't seem to fit very well the haunting cases in which the ghost's behavior is not always repetitive, and especially not in the unusual cases when the ghost seems to interact with the living observer. I say "unusual" because more typically the ghosts in hauntings seem oblivious to the living, and act like "dumb ghosts."

It may also have occurred to you that "retrocognition" may not necessarily mean that there is any residual energy, say on the Gettysburg battlefield, if the experiencer is actually looking back into a space-time location that is no longer present in Gettysburg today. Maybe it would be more appropriate to refer to such cases as involving a "time slip" (or time warp), as Evans (2002: 210-211) refers to it. Evans gives some fascinating examples, such as a case of an apparition in Avebury, England, of a village fair someone saw in recent times even though it had been abolished in 1850, and an old avenue of megaliths that had disappeared before 1800.

When I was in Avebury in 2008, I will confess to "imagining" that I was communicating with a long-gone stone workman as I stood by one of the standing stones. I asked him why they had put them there, and he said (I heard in my head), "The power of the stones will protect us." Now, just supposing that that exchange had any validity, it would seem to indicate a surviving spirit capable of interacting with me, and not just a "dumb ghost."

Nevertheless, back to the residual haunting theory (or frame), some analysts stick to the notion that there is something physical in the place itself. Gauld (1982: 250-252) considers Myers' theory, for example, that the dreams of the departed have somehow modified the space. This reminds me somewhat of Schwartz and Russek's *The Living Energy Universe* (1999), in which Gary Schwartz states that information is imprinted in walls, for example, based on sound waves that have bounced off it. Getting the information back out (like from a phonograph record) might be tricky.

In like manner, Evans (2002: 211-213) reports on geophysical theories that posit certain soils as facilitating paranormal information retention, such as the clay subsoil in East Anglia in the UK. Mark Nesbitt, author of the *Ghosts of Gettysburg* books, told me in an interview that he had found sources suggesting that there were more ghost reports from battlefields that contained a great deal of quartz. He likened it to the information function of quartz in a watch. I'm trying to keep my eyeballs level here, and I must say that I have no expertise that would entitle me either to support or to cast doubt upon this theory.

Evans (2002: 250) also discusses William Roll's idea that there can be a psi field of a house that magnetizes the residual information even after the consciousness that created it is no longer there. This sounds similar to Myers' concept of the dreams of the departed modifying a space.

Now, how about EVP (electronic voice phenomenon), although we are encroaching somewhat on the subject matter of Chapter Fourteen (physical effects)? I have interviewed Mark Nesbitt and also paranormal investigators Al Rauber and Garrett Husveth on whether EVP provides evidence for survival. All three of them have recorded what they consider to be very convincing voices on tape in allegedly haunted locations.

All three of these investigators think that the best recordings that contain clear voices (though nothing was audible during the recording) are very strong evidence for survival. Rauber and Husveth point out that although some scientists are not willing to be impressed, friends and relatives of the departed are sometimes thoroughly convinced. Be that as it may, the issue for us in this chapter is whether or not the voices are interactive, i.e. responsive to the investigator's questions.

At least in Mark Nesbitt's work with EVP, which I observed first hand, it would appear that they are interactive. Oftentimes the voices are so indistinct as to make it unclear whether an appropriate response is being given. For example, "Who was your commander here at Gettysburg?" may be followed by an unintelligible, gruff noise on the tape. I should clarify that

I heard no noise in the room at the time the response was being recorded on the tape. However, the very fact that something appeared on the tape just following the question suggests an interaction.

Summing up, ghosts (or apparitions) are apparent sensory experiences that seem not to be caused by any real physical stimulus, e.g. visions of people who disappear or seem transparent, sounds of footsteps when there is no one there, or smells from nonexistent cigars. Such experiences occur universally, although they are often given different cultural interpretations.

Once all other explanations are exhausted (waking dreams, illusions, hoaxes, etc.), one wonders if the remaining cases, especially the evidential ones (collective, or with paranormal info attached), represent contact with the spirit world. Even those parapsychologists and others who follow this logic to this point, however, have varying theories about the sources of apparitions and about whether they provide evidence for traveling consciousness (beyond the brain) or for life after death.

As with all the other phenomena we've been discussing, there are multiple possible frames. Don't despair; by the end we'll be able to draw these together, because there are many common threads. Next we'll look at paranormal physical effects (PK and psychic/spiritual healing), carrying forward the issue of whether there is anything really physical about the apparent reach of consciousness beyond the brain.

Chapter Fourteen

PHYSICAL EFFECTS (PK, HEALING)

In the last chapter we wondered whether people's experiences of ghosts or apparitions, if taken seriously, might provide any evidence for consciousness beyond the brain or for survival. Since some of these experiences seemed to involve physical effects, especially in poltergeist cases and in hauntings, you might say that we have already stolen some of the thunder from this chapter, which is also about physical effects.

Well, yes and no. We still have more to say about PK (psychokinesis) and about spiritual or psychic healing. Both of these subjects are dear to my heart, since I have had personal experiences with both of them. There's nothing like an experience, remember.

I should admit having a bias against the idea of there being spiritual evil, even though there seems to be plenty of it among the living. I mentioned before that Rogo didn't see evil as a very common theme among reliable first-hand apparition reports. Nevertheless, he did recognize that it seems to occur, including in demonic possession cases reported throughout the history of the Roman Catholic Church (Rogo, 1979: 204-229). One interesting physical aspect in demonic possession is levitation (floating up in the air), which has been reported fairly often in such cases, as with St. Theresa of Avila (Rogo, 1979:229). Other allegedly possessed people have reportedly experienced body bloating and being levitated and thrown up against the wall.

Levitation is a paranormal phenomenon that is hard for me to swallow. Nevertheless I encountered what seems to be a reliable case reported to me by a trustworthy witness, a student of mine at Gettysburg College. He and a few of his friends were playing around with a Ouija board when one of them was thrown back against the wall. Needless to say, the group was rather frightened, a reaction that grew over the next several days when a couple of them kept seeing lights flying about the room, and one of them became very psychic for about a week. For example, he told another guy in the group, "See those girls over there [who were out of earshot]? They're talking about [thus and so]." When they went over to verify the claim, they found that it was true.

I have not seen any people levitated, but I have apparently experienced the levitation of tables. I say apparently, because I still have my doubts. This is also called "table-tipping," and I reported on two observations of it from 1964 and 1999 in our book *Guided by Spirit* (Emmons and Emmons, 2003: 137-138).

In 1964 I attended a cast party after a play I was in. Two people set up a "rise, table, rise" game with four of us around a card table. To my great surprise the entire table floated up in the air about half a foot. It felt as if it were being buoyed up, as if by water, rather than being pulled or yanked. Everybody's hands were flat on top of the table, until I left it and dropped to my knees looking for strings, lifted legs, or anything irregular that might have been part of a hoax. I could detect nothing, and the table was still up in the air. However, I still thought it was some kind of a trick, because I had seen the two organizers whisper something to each other over the center of the table before we started.

In 1999 I was part of a table-tipping demonstration class involving Anne Gehman, a prominent spirit medium for whom I have the greatest respect. Five of us around a card table weren't getting far, except for what I call a slight "Ouija-board effect," or rocking back and forth that could be explained simply as an unconscious pressure from our hands. We were not achieving lift-off. But then Anne came by and placed her hands on top of the corner of the table to the right of mine. The rest of her body was clearly away from the table. Darned if it didn't float up after a couple of seconds about six inches from that corner only, with that same buoying effect I had experienced 35 years earlier. It stayed there for about ten or twenty seconds, then fell rather quickly, but it rose up again with Anne's hands still on the table. After another ten or twenty seconds she left our table, and it stayed up for a few more seconds without her but then collapsed, never to rise again.

The next day I had a lengthy discussion with a very reliable observer who had been sitting across the table from me. He pointed out that Anne had had no way to get leverage in order to lift the table in any normal fashion, because the table legs were on the very corners of the table, and her hands were entirely on top. He also thought that the rising of the table had felt like a buoying effect rather than a yanking or pulling. There had also been several other students in the class sitting in nearby chairs checking for funny stuff, and nobody had said anything.

Interestingly Stephen Braude, philosophy professor at University of Maryland, Baltimore Campus, told me in an interview that he had had a similar experience in graduate school. He called it a "table-up séance." From his skeptical, materialist perspective at the time, he watched what seemed to be an impossible event as the table tipped. He said: they were not jokers, it was his table, it was daylight, etc., nothing suspicious. Much later, after he had a job and was a tenured professor, he knew that he would have to confront the experience and other apparent anomalies that it represented in his mind. There's nothing like an experience.

For me, also a "materialist," and an atheist at the time, my conversion experience came in my sophomore year at Gannon College, when I took a class in psychology from the late John Fleming, who devoted a section of the class to parapsychology. This was in 1962, two years before my table-tipping experience (Emmons and Emmons, 2003: 94-95). I was fascinated by the evidence he presented for ESP and PK (psychokinesis or mind-over-matter). It didn't fit my materialistic explanation of the universe. However, instead of thinking, "It can't be, therefore it isn't (the normal-science attitude)," I thought, "It seems to be, surprisingly, so I'd better check it out."

The following summer I did my own PK experiment by rolling dice 200,000 times, attempting to influence the dice to come up with a 5 on each die. I used a dice cup and recorded all the data by hand. It wasn't a controlled experiment in a laboratory setting, just a way of satisfying my curiosity addiction. I got between 1½ and 2 percent more fives than expected by chance, the odds of which are billions to one against for a sample that large.

I have to say that Prof. Fleming had a psychology major (I was a language major) test my dice in a lab, rolling them in a mechanical device and recording the results. They actually produced a bit less than the expected number of fives, indicating that the dice, if anything, were slightly biased against my target, rather than for it. He also sent my results to J.B. Rhine, the famous parapsychologist, who responded that my data were typical of such experiments, showing, for example, classic decline effects (psi-missing) at the end of a long run. Rhine even sent me some Las Vegas dice that were well-balanced, unlike the "drugstore dice" I had been using. I tried them out for a while, but did not get significant results.

Keep in mind that my adventures with dice do not belong in the annals of parapsychological research. Nowadays, in any case, PK is tested with random number generators etc. (more on this shortly). They merely represent a significant experience in my life that made me more open to the exploration of anomalies. Even though I had never thought of myself as psychic or anything of that ilk, it gradually dawned on me that such things were apparently possible, even for myself.

I had always scoffed when my mother told me that she couldn't wear watches because she magnetized them, and they stopped. Surely, I thought, the human body can't create enough electromagnetic energy to do that. However, for the past few decades I have experienced something similar. When I have worn self-winding mechanical watches previously worn by my dad, they end up losing time in odd ways, especially when I am pressed for time. Also, the one I have now will sometimes keep perfect time all night, then stop when I put it on in the morning, without setting it, winding it, or doing anything else to the stem. Is this a PK effect? By the way, I finally have bought a quartz watch, which is not affected, so that I can actually tell what time it is without getting out my cell phone.

There have been other such apparent PK effects in my life, most of which are out of my conscious control, although I did on two occasions consciously get my "psychic watch" to stop and then start again in a few minutes (with a witness, who was rather disturbed by it). I also found recently that both Penelope and I were able to stare at a little 1940s Christmas ornament lamp shade (called "Whirl Glo") and apparently make it move around from our thoughts instead of from the heat of the Christmas light, which I had switched off (we were careful not to breathe on it or to create air currents in any other way). I thought we had discovered a way to demonstrate our PK to the world, but we could not do this again after a few times. And then the skeptic in me made me doubt that the effect was genuine in the first place.

If any of these experiences of mine are valid, they appear to represent PK by the living, which harkens back to the poltergeist material in the last chapter. In some other of my experiences, however, the physical effects might represent at least some influence from the spirit world, which relates to what we said about hauntings.

Shortly after my father died in 1996, I noticed that six remote control devices in his house had the batteries die all within a few days of each other. I thought that that was just a bit too much of a coincidence. It reminded me of clocks stopping after a person's death ("The clock stopped, never to go again, when the old man died.").

Shortly after Penelope's aunt died, we were staying in her house to visit, and we experienced flickering of the lights in the kitchen for no apparent reason around 3:00 or 4:00 o'clock in the morning. The family wondered if it might not be because she used to raid the refrigerator at that time of day.

A few years ago I got a phone call in Lily Dale, NY (our summer residence) from a member of the First Spiritualist Church of Erie to tell me that a fellow member of the church had just died. For a second or two I couldn't place the name, but then I blurted out, "Oh, Pearl!", a particularly sweet woman I admired very much. At the very moment I had my realization, the ceiling light bulb in the room popped and burned out.

As you may know, this is rare, because bulbs generally blow out when you turn them on and send a surge of electricity through, not when they have been on for a time. I wondered if I wasn't getting a message from Pearl, although I suppose it could also have been my own PK . . . or just a normal electrical phenomenon of course.

There have been other physical effects in our Lily Dale house. Shortly after Penelope's mother died a few pictures fell off the wall (oddly), as well as a commemorative plate with an image of the flagship Niagara on it, for which her mother had worked on a fundraiser to restore the ship. There were several other plates up there, none of which came down. In about the same place as the plate and pictures, I took a photograph of Penelope that showed an odd double image over her (she was still visible underneath) of what looked like a billowy curtain fabric with cross-hatched lines of corded material. I could not find anything in the house that looked like that.

All of these examples are what are referred to as "spontaneous cases", rather than laboratory cases. Also, my dice experiments are of little consequence due to the lack of controls and to the outmoded methodology. See Mayer (2007: 241-247) for a review of the extensive research done at the Princeton Engineering Anomalies Research laboratories by Robert Jahn and Brenda Dunne, beginning in 1977. Their most sophisticated methodology involved people using their intention to influence the output of a random number generator. The cumulative effect of all of their experimental trials shows odds of 100 billion to one against mere chance.

Back in Chapter Five on skepticism, I referred to physicist Michiu Kaku's (2008: 92) critique of Jahn and Dunne's research, in which he wrote that "the effects are quite tiny . . . no more than a few parts per ten thousand on average." I also pointed out that he chose to ignore the fact that the statistical analysis of the cumulative deviation over a very large number of trials shows a very significant deviation from chance. There is also much more to the story, as they have done many studies to identify factors in the experimental conditions and in the subjects that correlate with success (Jahn and Dunne, 2011).

Also, let us not forget the substantive significance of their research (as opposed to the statistical significance). If there is evidence for our conscious intention being able to create a physical effect, no matter how small, on a random number generator, or on the roll of dice, this may show the influence of consciousness at a distance. Or it might indicate that our consciousness can travel to a place outside the brain and have a physical impact there.

Braude (1997: 3-5, 228-321), however, argues that such laboratory experiments, with their emphasis on quantitative data, are problematic because they are artificial and don't really explain why PK occurs; nor have they convinced the skeptics. Braude (1997: 63-154) would like to see more analysis of large-scale PK, as with the cases of Daniel Douglas Home (1833-1886), who was famous for levitating himself, and of Eusapia Palladino (1854-1918), who levitated tables. Palladino certainly cheated some of the time, but not all of the time, he says; and the "evidence of large-scale PK [is] respectable" (Braude: 1997: 154), i.e., well documented.

One type of physical-effect evidence that is probably less respectable is the "apport." In Spiritualist circles this is known as a "gift from spirit." "Apport" is a French word for something brought in, or a contribution. Sometimes people have reported objects like rings or flowers showing up on the table in a séance. I have had several people report to me that objects would disappear and then reappear elsewhere, such as a lost camera that unexpectedly showed up right in the middle of the dining-room table after people had looked high and low for it. In another case, a wedding ring showed up mysteriously on the top of a door frame. Of course such cases are typically difficult to verify, occurring spontaneously and under anything but controlled laboratory conditions.

This is another topic that tests my threshold of eye-rolling. Nevertheless, I have had a few experiences that might fall in this category. One morning I found two small objects side by side on top of a wicker chest in my office at home. One was a very old style of paper clip, probably at least 50 years old. The other was a buffalo nickel in very good condition. I know that there were some coins like this in my late father's coin collection, but that was well packed away, and there is no way that I would have had one in my current coins and have dropped it there. Using my imagination, and thinking in terms of synchronicities that might have some meaning, I wondered if my father was trying to tell me, "Don't get clipped; don't take any wooden nickels." I know that's a stretch, but I am still at a loss to explain how those objects got there.

My favorite example of an apparent apport is the case of the "psychic teeth" that we reported in *Guided by Spirit* (Emmons and Emmons, 2003: 129). Four molars showed up one day in our sink among some silverware. Looking for a logical explanation, I accused household members of dropping them there out of some old container with wisdom teeth in them or something. No. I even imagined that workmen who had just finally fixed the water filtration system (after ten visits) had found plastic teeth in the basement by a filtration unit and had dropped them in the sink upstairs. Penelope noted that the whole repair process had been symbolically "like pulling teeth."

My guess that the teeth were plastic was based on some neat round holes drilled in them, that I thought might serve for threading them on a necklace. To my surprise, when I took the teeth to my dentist, he told me that they were genuine teeth, perhaps from a teenage girl (no such person in our house). He pointed out that there were also file marks, which along with the holes indicated to him that they might have been used to demonstrate tooth structure at a dental school.

I love bizarre cases like this. I was left with two possible explanations, and I don't know which is worse. A normal explanation might be that someone walked in off the street and put the teeth in our sink for no apparent reason. A paranormal one might be that one of Penelope's deceased grandfathers, who sometimes worked with teeth in his capacity as a medical doctor, and who Penelope believes communicates with her mentally on health issues, dropped them there as a joke about how the repair work was "like pulling teeth."

Another type of physical effect that is considered, at least sometimes, as paranormal, is spiritual/psychic healing. My single favorite treatment of such healing is by Jane Katra in *Miracles of Mind: Exploring Nonlocal Consciousness and Spiritual Healing* (Targ and Katra, 1998). See also Larry Dossey ("Compassion and Healing" in Simon, 2008: 55-56) for a discussion of nonlocal healing, including double-blind studies of praying for strangers. Marilyn Schlitz and Dean Radin have a chapter on "Prayer and Intention in Distant Healing: Assessing the Evidence" in Simon (2008: 387-402). Some studies contain interesting protocols that show measurable changes in the physiology of a target individual that correlate with the intentions of another person down the hall.

Evidence in such studies is highly suggestive, in spite of sometimes small sample sizes and the difficulty of eliminating outside contamination, e.g. from healing intentions and prayers coming from elsewhere. Dean Radin told me in an interview that he has increasingly tended to publish in alternative medical journals rather than in parapsychology journals due to the implications of such research for practical applications in medicine.

Based on my participant observation of healing and healers over the past fifteen years, including my involvement as a student in five different courses on Spiritualist church healing and reiki, I can see quite a variety of techniques and philosophies involved. Perhaps the most general belief is that a loving, compassionate intent is important on the part of the healer. I would also emphasize an awareness and accepting attitude on the part of the subject, although this is not absolutely necessary. However, there are also many specific healing modalities, indeed rituals, practiced by various groups.

For one thing, some techniques focus on proximity to the body and the stimulation of the body's energy field (aura, chakras, etc.). On the other hand, healing practices may be done at any distance. There is also a difference between psychic healing (at whatever distance) and spiritual healing, in the sense that the latter may involve appealing to some spiritual being to do the work.

Let's take myself as an example of a healer, and I do volunteer as a healer in Spiritualist churches. First of all, as a social scientist I agree with James McClenon's (2002) ritual healing theory, according to which spiritual healing in all cultures depends upon a combination of hypnotizability and placebo effect. I can see how this applies to healing in church, in that the peaceful, relaxing atmosphere is conducive to a hypnotic effect, and in that people come to the healing benches usually with a belief in the process (aiding the placebo effect). Knowing this makes it easy for me to feel useful as a healer without wondering if there is really anything spiritual or psychic going on.

However, in addition to my sociological perspective on healing, I entertain the notion that there is a spiritual component (if there's not, no harm done). I have a "spiritual healing team" of five deceased humans who I imagine are doing the healing work for me, between my hands and the body of the person sitting on the bench. I often get intuitive notions of what the person needs and move my hands based on these notions.

I also can feel some kind of energy (which is difficult to describe) between my hands and the sitter. One time I asked my spirit team what the sitter needed, and I heard (in my head), "She needs to believe." I also got the message that I should hold my hands a few inches from her face a little longer than usual. After the healing service, the woman came up to me and said that she could really feel a lot of energy from my hands, especially when they were by her face. I took this as a sign that I should believe in the process myself.

Is this another example of my PK tendencies (added to my experiences with dice and with my watches referred earlier in this chapter)? And if so, is there some kind of paranormal physical energy emanating from my body, or is it just another kind of nonlocal connection or entanglement? By now you'll remember that we've asked this same question in several other chapters about whether there is anything physical extending beyond the brain or body.

Russell Targ (2004: 4) says that distant healing is an outflow of information to anywhere, as opposed to remote viewing, which is an inflow of information from anywhere. I still want to know if that "inflow of information" is a physical, spatial movement of some kind, or just entanglement at a distance.

Targ (2004: 8-24) goes on to discuss "the physics of miracles" in terms of added imaginary spatial dimensions, physics as the geometry of curved spaces, and Buddhist concepts of logic that are compatible with quantum physics, in which things can be both true and not true, and also neither true nor not true. Suffice it to say that things may not be what they seem.

Rogo (1979: 133) thought that PK might be produced somehow by "cooling the atmosphere [which] would release a ready source of energy, which could be redirected by and as PK." He noted that cold spots have often been reported in hauntings. For other discussions of possible physics explanations for paranormal physical effects, see Roderick H. Boes (The Physics of Encounter, 2009), and Lynne McTaggert (The Field, 2001).

PENELOPE'S COMMENTS:

Starting in the 1980s I was trained in Reiki, therapeutic touch, polarity, qigong, crystal healing, hands-on healing as used by Spiritualist churches, and other healing modalities. Sometimes people appeared to be healed or have less pain from the love they received. For this chapter I will choose to speak of my own personal healing(s). It might be useful to the reader.

In 1980 I was "burned out." My doctor had diagnosed that I had adrenal exhaustion, presumably brought on by designing and building a passive solar home from the ground up, holding two jobs, having three children, and raising, canning, freezing, cooking organic vegetarian food (in a time that it wasn't available in supermarkets). I had also developed a cyst on my left ovary. Instead of surgery, I chose to go to the Himalayan Institute in Honesdale, PA to see if I could heal by participating in their ten day Combined Therapy program. For more information on this, see *Guided by Spirit* (Emmons and Emmons, 2003: 55-56).

While there I learned about myself, especially in their Science of Breath lab. I also began yoga, a new form of meditation, biofeedback, and yoga psychology, and practiced many forms of cleansing, nutrition and homeopathy. The process did not help me avoid surgery a few years later; but it did set the stage for how to use, not abuse, my body as a tool for healing, mediumship, being conscious and knowing.

Later in the 1980s I had viral encephalitis. Dr Jesse Stoff, an endocrinologist and immunology specialist, helped me to heal. He used his knowledge, backed by his insight and some tests, along with input from myself as well as from a nutritionist, an acupuncturist, and a psycho-neuro-immunologist in the healing process.

At one point I expressed my disappointment and critical thoughts about myself because there were some vitamins I had bought but just would not take. I didn't know if I was blocked, stubborn, wasteful of the money they cost, or rebellious . . . yet I regularly took some and not others. Soon after that visit he had an opportunity to visit the different laboratories/factories where they were made. He discovered a peaceful atmosphere in the places that made the ones I would take, but a chaotic, unfriendly setting where the ones I would not swallow were produced. For me this was a lesson in trusting my gut, instead of being critical of myself. At one point Jesse felt I needed even more than he could offer, and he suggested that I visit the Ayurvedic clinic in Lancaster, MA.

At that clinic I was told that I had a highly sensitive nervous system and was called a reishi (knower or seer) in the Ayurvedic tradition. This insight combined with the compassion I had for others following years of my own illness allowed me to trust myself as a channel for healing. I came to realize that my attitude and intention to heal the body/mind/spirit was more important than the particular modality (e.g. reiki or therapeutic touch).

Chapter Fifteen

SPIRIT MEDIUMSHIP

Back in Chapter Thirteen we looked at ghost experiences for possible clues regarding the mysterious question of survival. As you can imagine, spirit mediumship contains very similar issues, because it is another alleged way of communicating with the dead. Is mediumship just a mental delusion or hallucination, a hoax, or at best ESP (all possibilities for ghost experiences)? Even if we find evidential cases, do these indicate survival or "just" (super) ESP? If it's ESP, does this mean an extension of consciousness in some quasi-physical way, or "just" quantum entanglement at a distance?

Nevertheless, for many, both parapsychologists and participants in spirit mediumship, mediumship is one of the best, if not the very best, types of evidence for survival. One of the best overview treatments of this evidence is still Alan Gauld's *Mediumship and Survival* (1982). One profound comment he makes is that, "If there were no evidence at all for ESP, the case for survival could well be much stronger than it is" (Gauld, 1982: 7).

This pretty much sums up the problem. In other words, if a spirit medium acts as if she is speaking to you on behalf of your deceased relative, and gives you lots of information she couldn't possibly know about both the relative and you, you would be tempted to declare that she must be in touch with the spirit world. And so you might think, especially if you had no concept of ESP. In fact, as sympathetic as I am with spirit mediumship, it astonishes me sometimes how undiscerning people can be in this regard. This is because I am both a scientist and a Spiritualist (operating with dual frames).

As Gauld (1982: 15) points out, the "central dilemma" is that a medium might know anything from any source of knowledge at any time in any place, under the concept of super-ESP (ESP with no limit). The problem is that we can't really test what the limits of ESP might be, if any. This leaves us with the strategy of becoming detectives, looking for who has the motivation to communicate paranormally, for example.

Perhaps the most useful kind of spirit-mediumship communication for determining who has the motivation to communicate is the type known as "drop-in communicators," a term coined by Ian Stevenson, who is better known for his work on reincarnation (Gauld, 1982: 58-59). In such cases the information seems to come from a spirit whom neither the medium nor the sitter (the person coming for a reading) knows anything about. Such cases can be very difficult to verify for obvious reasons, but they are important ones, because they imply that the information came from the spirit, the only party apparently motivated to focus on the information.

Some such cases have come from séances, in which the people in the circle have invited spirits to appear, and up comes someone who died before any of the people present was born, to tell about having lost a leg or dying in an air battle, which information is later verified after considerable research.

Somewhat related are "obsession and possession" cases (Gauld, 1982: 147), in which a spirit seems to enter the mind and/or body of the medium (obsession leaving the medium in greater control than possession). Penelope and I (Emmons and Emmons, 2003: 74-76) reported on a case like this, in which Penelope experienced being "obsessed" apparently by the spirit of Union officer Joshua Chamberlain in July, 1995 on Little Round top, at the scene of the Battle of Gettysburg, on the anniversary of the battle (1863).

Not only were there several evidential aspects to the communication (for example, her feeling pains in hip and ankle, the same places Chamberlain had been wounded), but in 2001 I received an email from a woman who had had a very similar experience of Joshua Chamberlain trying to "take her over." This woman had seen me on a national TV show talking about ghosts, but she knew nothing about Penelope's experience (this was two years before the book came out).

I have received hundreds, if not thousands, of communications from people based on that TV show ("Ghosts of Gettysburg"), but this woman was the only person ever to talk to me about obsession/possession rather than just a regular ghost experience, and she reported the same spirit Penelope had, also on the anniversary of the battle. We found out later that Chamberlain, when alive, often revisited the Gettysburg battlefield on the anniversary of the battle. These independent experiences of obsession might indicate that his spirit is still motivated to explore the battlefield after death.

Aside from the strategy of trying to determine what source the message is coming from, which in the case of drop-in communicators would appear to be someone in the spirit world, there is also the issue of whether the medium would be capable of gathering the information. Previously we considered the concept of super-ESP, which might indicate that spirit mediums might be able to gather information from any time or place at all, if there is no limit to what ESP can do.

Nevertheless, the question remains what would cause the medium to focus on some particular set of information among limitless possibilities. This combination of capability and motivation is especially challenged in a group of communications known as "the cross-correspondences." From 1901 to 1932 a large number of these communications were recorded through spirit mediums associated with the Society for Psychical Research in England (Gauld, 1982: 77-89). Although the analysis is very complicated, it appears that certain combinations of messages make sense only when pieced together from the work of multiple mediums working in isolation. It has been suggested that deceased paranormal researchers, like Myers, Sidgwick, and Gurney created these puzzles after their death, sending partial messages back to each of various mediums, whose work then had to be compared by others (Gauld, 1982: 78; Targ, 2004: 102; Saltmarsh, 2004).

One simplified example for purposes of illustration would be as follows. Suppose that medium A states that in the home library of deceased Prof. X there is a book on the third bookshelf from the left, second shelf from the top, fourth book from the left, and that on page 13 line four there is a particular sentence. Medium B identifies another passage somewhere else, and medium C a third passage. Then a parapsychologist combines these sentences, and they make sense together, saying something relevant to the life of another parapsychologist, deceased. The cross-correspondences contain many such examples. They suggest that the source of the communication is the deceased parapsychologist, because no one else involved in the communication can see the entire picture.

Gauld (1982: 90-101) also discusses other elements that make the communication through spirit mediums more likely to be from the spirit world. One set of these has to do with the medium imitating convincingly the gestures, mannerisms, turns of phrase etc. of the deceased. Chinese spirit mediums sometimes imitate the gestures, mannerisms and dialect of the deceased (Emmons, 1982: 187), although I did not see this in the particular case I observed in Hong Kong. Penelope broke out in a rash one time that imitated the rash the spirit had had in life.

Another such feature is "xenoglossy," speaking in the language of the spirit, especially when the medium is not familiar with the language (Gauld, 1982: 101). Russell Targ (2004: 102-103) refers to a message sent through a spiritual healer in Seattle apparently from his deceased daughter Elisabeth Targ in Russian, in which Elisabeth had been fluent. Laine Crosby, a medium interviewed for this study, told me that she received material in French on one occasion, and she had to write it down phonetically, not knowing French.

As you can see, what these elements have in common (gestures, mannerisms, xenoglossy) is that they go beyond knowing something about the spirit. They involve "being" the spirit, or as someone has said, "knowing how" rather than merely "knowing." ESP (super or not) would seem to involve merely knowing rather than knowing how.

In his interview with us in 2008, Russell Targ gave us a case that exemplifies "knowing how," a case that he called "the gold standard" for evidence for survival. It involves a chess game between a living chess grandmaster and allegedly a deceased one (assisted by a spirit medium).

There are two articles in the *Journal of the Society for Psychical Research* (Eisenbeiss and Hassler, 2006; Neppe, 2007) that analyze the match in detail. In summary, this is what happened. Eisenbeiss enlisted living grandmaster Viktor Korchnoi to play a chess game against the deceased Hungarian master Geza Maroczy (1870-1951), the latter having been contacted by automatic-writing medium Robert Rollans (1914-1993) in 1985. The game lasted from 1985-1993, requiring a total of 47 moves. It usually took about ten days before Rollans received a move from Maroczy. "Rollans felt a tickle in his body and then knew he had to go . . . write down a new message [in algebraic notation, e.g. "e4" for pawn to king four] . . . . At one instance he related that he was taking a shower when he sensed that tickle and had to cut it short" (Eisnebeiss and Hassler, 2006: 67).

In the end, Korchnoi won, but the game was in doubt throughout the middle, which was played in the compact style of Maroczy, who nevertheless was not up on recent developments in end play and lost the game. Russell Targ took the score of the game to his (now deceased) brother-in-law, U.S. former world chess champion, Bobby Fischer. Fischer said that the game was clearly high level, and that anybody who could go 47 moves with Korchnoi had to be playing at a grandmaster level.

Targ pointed out to me that what makes this a "gold standard" piece of evidence, of course, is that Rollans, who scarcely knew anything about chess, was hardly competent to play such a game, and since this was before there were computers clever enough to play at this level, there was really no way for him to cheat (the case was investigated thoroughly for fraud). Rollans also brought through lots of obscure information about Maroczy, which was scored 94% accurate, but this aspect could be construed as ESP. "Knowing how" is better evidence for survival than "knowing."

Before leaving this case, which I must admit is my favorite, and I agree with Russell Targ that it's apparently the gold standard; I have to say that not everyone is convinced by it. One of my interviewees for this study, a social scientist who could probably be called an open-minded skeptic, said that he didn't think it was remarkable evidence at all. His reasoning? He said that we just don't know the limits of the human mind. Hmm. That seems rather glib to me, but of course he's right. How can we explain what an idiot savant does? But of course the same goes for the best spirit mediums. Whether we interpret what they do one way or the other may have more to do with our own "frame" than it does with the evidence, a point I have made earlier in this book of course.

Some other aspects of spirit mediums' work are more problematic, according to Gauld (1982: 114), who thinks that the "controls" or spirit guides used frequently by mediums to contact other spirits seem to be merely secondary personalities of the medium. In some of the classic cases, Gauld states that the controls are apparently fictitious, with names such as Phinuit, Chlorine, and Julius Caesar (a personality who seemed very unlike the original). Gauld (1982: 119-138) also talks about there being lots of "rubbish" mixed into even generally good communications, suggesting that the medium's personality is often coloring or adding to the work.

I think that these points about how spirit mediums may be adding their own spin, even if they are getting something from the spirit world, can be related to some things Dean Radin told me in his interview in 2007. He pointed out that mediumship is typically a healing ritual for the sitter, and the medium is motivated to present information as if it were from a surviving spirit in order to relieve anxiety and grief on the part of the sitter. Of course as a sociologist I am well aware of this function, which we talk about in *Guided by Spirit* (2003: 143-177) in terms of healing, grief counseling etc.

For Dean Radin, the point is that the medium may be dressing up as a spirit message information received through ESP (he doesn't like the term super-ESP, since he thinks that it implies that usual ESP is not very potent, but in fact the material in remote viewing can be very detailed and accurate). He thinks that it is easier to believe that mediums' messages are ESP, because remote viewing can be very strong. Because of quantum entanglement, information can be known at any distance or time separation.

Nevertheless, Radin thinks that spirit mediumship is the most direct evidence that may indicate survival of consciousness beyond death.

As Senior Scientist and Laboratory Director at IONS (Institute of Noetic Sciences), he is more involved in remote viewing, and he thinks that remote-viewing researchers are more likely to think that ESP explains mediumship, whereas those who study mediums are likely to think in terms of survival.

For those who want more detailed treatment of spirit medium research, I highly recommend Stephen F. Braude's *Immortal Remains: The Evidence for Life after Death* (2003), which discusses very smartly the classic cases of spirit mediumship, as well as reincarnation and OBEs/NDEs. See also Gary Schwartz's *The Afterlife Experiments* (2002) for a laboratory approach to mediumship as well as a discussion of various interpretations of evidential material (is it survival?).

In our own work, the spirit mediumship part of *Chinese Ghosts and ESP* (Emmons, 1982) was written more from the perspective of a social scientist and amateur parapsychologist. I was more likely to think of the evidential examples of mediumship I observed as some sort of ESP. By the time of *Guided by Spirit: A Journey into the Mind of the Medium* (Emmons and Emmons, 2003), however, I was thinking more like a Spiritualist (but still as a social scientist), and I was more open to the survival explanation. So of course was Penelope.

More importantly, *Guided by Spirit* is largely a phenomenological study. In other words, it looks at the explanations spirit mediums give for what they do. This is a very important methodological point. Instead of just doing "objective" studies of spirit mediums, in which they are tested in a laboratory, or their messages are checked for the validity of the content, why not also ask spirit mediums what they think is going on? What a concept!

Indeed, because of the impasse in consciousness studies, in which neuroscientists cannot actually "see" or "locate" our consciousness objectively, it seems important to examine the subjective experiences we have with our own consciousness. In the final section of this chapter, Penelope will discuss her own understanding of spirit mediumship and what it might tell us about survival, based upon her own experiences.

PENELOPE'S COMMENTS:

Many times in the past fifty years I have said: I think this (paranormal) information comes just because I can know anything by becoming still and knowing. Yet just as often I decide it is telepathy, or being a clairvoyant rishi (a knower or seer). Then I am talking as a medium with a sitter, and I get goose bumps with strong feelings of love or elation to be talking with the person, an intensity of devotion beyond what I have felt personally, or occasionally a fear or physical pain sensation that comes out of the blue and has nothing to do with who I am. Unless some scientist figures out how to measure these spontaneous sensations/emotions, how can we detect the differences among telepathy, clairvoyance, and now-moment communication with a spiritual being?

As we were researching mediumship some years ago I came to the conclusion it was ESP, just knowing. Then I went to the Forest Temple service and asked a woman if she would like a message. These are short, public messages without much feedback. My eyes were draw to a woman's wedding ring. I sensed a spirit of someone standing too close behind me. (If someone violated your personal space by moving within 3 inches behind you, you would know it.) I "knew" it was a man; it was like my becoming the spirit. Yet I still retained my personal self, so I silently asked who it was and saw a clairvoyant image of silver with the letters R. R. in fancy script. That instantly faded, and I felt swamped with love for the woman I was speaking to. As much love and devotion as I have ever felt in my life. Then I heard, external to me, the man crack a joke that he came to Lily Dale today without her dragging him. I thought he called her Angel Eyes, and again I felt intense love for her. I so longed to hold her close instead of remaining at the front of the group as I did. I then clairvoyantly viewed an image of a swan on a lake and heard him say that he was pleased with the choices she was making. Again I was flooded with love for her, felt pleasure from looking at her. I experienced all of this, and told it to her in less time than it has taken me to write it. Total time . . . under three minutes, total love . . . immeasurable.

After the service the woman came up to me and expressed how important a healing those few words were. Her husband had died the past year, and today was their anniversary. She then verified the precise language and images I had received. A year before she had asked her husband to come to Lily Dale with her as her anniversary present. Now she was tickled he had come from another place without complaint a year later! His name was Ralph Rosenblad, and two silver soup spoons had his father's initials, for Rolf Rosenblad. Since his death she had decided to sell the home they had lived in for years and buy a condo west of town on a lake. What had helped her make the decision was a swan she had seen gliding by when she viewed the property. Since then she had moved and often wondered what he would think about her selling the home of their life together. She said her name was Angelina, and she had been feeling so lonesome on her first wedding anniversary without him, yet now she felt so loved and treasured by him.

While I may have used ESP (clairvoyance and telepathy), I think his spirit was also present. I had never before walked in another's shoes experiencing love beyond measure. What a healing gift to all three of us!

Charlie has asked me to provide an "insider's" point of view or frame. In sharing my experiences with spirit mediumship, another example stands out to me because the spirit consciousness appeared to be having a present-moment conversation with me in a private reading, as well as with the "sitter." As I meditated before the woman arrived I heard that I should go outside and cut a rose for her. I did so. It was a peace rose. Then when Maria, whom I did not know before, arrived, the spirit first commented on how I was inappropriately dressed. I was wearing orange socks. She began to describe herself: she would wear silk stockings and be certain the seams were straight. She would sit with her back straight and not cross-legged like I was. Her tone of voice was a reprimand for not being lady-like. She went on to describe herself as being like Queen Elizabeth's cousin, a lady, and she showed me herself even with a similar purse on her arm. Then I heard the name Ileana and thought about a picture I had seen in the past of the Tsar of Russia's family. Next I had an image of

South America, and said Argentina. The spirit said the name Alexandra, (at this point I thought of my granddaughter who has that name, but I just said that she was talking about Alexandra). She showed me a picture of Carlow College in Pittsburgh, PA where another daughter of mine had gone to school, and I heard the word "convent." I shared the thought of Pittsburgh and a convent.

At this point I asked the sitter, Maria, if this description made any sense to her. She answered yes, so I went on with a message from this spirit to her. It mostly involved the fact that she was sorry but understood her choices in going west (Colorado), getting married, choosing a different way of life. And the two of them had never said goodbye. She wanted to bestow her blessing, belatedly, onto Maria and to say, "Peace be with you." As the spirit withdrew from the room she told me to give the (peace) rose to Maria to take with her.

Maria said that it all made sense. The spirit was the former Princess Ileana of Romania, who was literally the cousin of Queen Elizabeth of England and related also to the Tsar of Russia. The princess emigrated to Argentina because of the politics of World War Two and eventually ended up in Pittsburgh as the head of an Eastern Orthodox convent. At that point she had changed her name from Ileana to Mother Alexandra. She became Maria's godmother and wanted Maria to switch from a Roman Catholic convent to her own. Disagreement over this issue led to an unresolved tension in their relationship. The spirit communication in this reading amounted to a reconciliation after death.

[Additional comment from Charlie:] We both found it interesting that Maria accepted the accuracy and detail of the reading without amazement (after all, Penelope was just doing her job). The parapsychologist in me finds this case amazingly evidential. After all, what were the odds that Maria's godmother was actually Queen Elizabeth's cousin, not to mention all the other details? However, because all of the information in the reading was known by the sitter (Maria), a parapsychologist would say that it could have been "merely" a case of telepathy (Penelope reading Maria's mind) rather than a conversation with a departed spirit. Spiritualists would tend to frame it as the latter.

The sociologist in me knows that the most important thing about the reading was that it had the function of helping Maria come to peace with her important unresolved disagreement with her godmother. However, I also think it is important to take Penelope's experience seriously. Phenomenologically, from the medium's perspective, it is important to note that the reading felt like a real conversation with another intelligence. This type of evidence for survival is also important.

Chapter Sixteen

REINCARNATION

The last type of evidence for us to consider for survival or life after death is reincarnation. We have already looked at some skeptical, even dismissive attitudes about reincarnation in Chapter 5 on skepticism. Perhaps there is some general cultural underpinning for the rejection of claims about reincarnation in the U.S., given that only about 20% of Americans believe in reincarnation. Both a Harris poll in 2009 and a Gallup poll in 2005 came up with 20%; compared to 21% in 2007 and 2005 in previous Harris polls; and 25% in 2001, 22% in 1996, 27% in 1994, and 21% in 1990 in previous Gallup polls.

One example of the dismissive attitude referred to in Chapter Five is Edwards's (2002: 7) statement that after a fair presentation of arguments for reincarnation, "I have tried to show that this evidence is worthless." His reasons for rejecting it include, "We have enormous evidence that the mind or consciousness cannot exist without the brain" (Edwards, 2002: 8). As you can see from other material so far in this book, some researchers would beg to differ.

Of course, more important than acceptance or rejection of findings is an atmosphere that allows research to continue. Ian Stevenson (1997B) thanked Dean Thomas Hunter at the University of Virginia for defending his right to conduct research on reincarnation, in spite of being very skeptical about it. Stevenson was well aware of the mainstream scientific opposition to his research, and in *Where Reincarnation and Biology Intersect* (1997B: xiii), he wrote that it was necessary for serious researchers to read the details of 225 cases he presented in a longer book on the same subject

(*Reincarnation and Biology*, 1997A) before expressing "an opinion about my conclusions."

Opposition to the idea of reincarnation comes not only from the mainstream scientific community but also from some religious communities. According to the Harris poll referred to above, belief in reincarnation was less in people of Christian backgrounds than in the population as a whole. Gauld (1982: 164) stated that Anglo-American Spiritualists have generally been opposed to the idea of reincarnation. From my research I can report that the National Spiritualist Association of Churches has relaxed its position from being opposed to believing in reincarnation to letting people decide on their own. Most Spiritualists I have encountered (and my church is a nonaffiliated, non-NSAC church) are more likely to accept reincarnation than not.

I don't know how many Spiritualists might have second thoughts about reincarnation because of the apparent contradiction in trying to contact people in the spirit world if they have perhaps already reincarnated and become another person. However, I do know that Chinese in Hong Kong are concerned about this. Some spirit mediums with Buddhist tendencies (and therefore with a belief in reincarnation) will ask how long the spirit has been dead, and if the sitter says it's been many years, the medium may decline to try to contact the spirit, saying, "Oh, she/he is probably reincarnated already."

Of course the late Ian Stevenson is not the only researcher who takes seriously what he cautiously called "cases suggestive of reincarnation." Gauld, for example, in his overview book on *Mediumship and Survival: A Century of Investigations* (1982: 187), considers Stevenson's evidence to be good and tentatively supportive of the idea of reincarnation, although it deserves further research (of course; this is all one hopes for). Likewise, Becker (*Paranormal Experience and Survival of Death*, 1993: 35) concludes that the data suggest that at least some "dying people are reborn later in other human bodies."

Support for the usefulness of research on reincarnation comes sometimes from surprising quarters. Perennial debunker Carl Sagan (*The*

Demon-Haunted World, 1997A) said that children's memories of past lives is one of three claims in parapsychology that is worth serious study. This does not surprise me all that much, however, because when I did my research on UFO investigators (Emmons, 1997), I thought that Carl Sagan was a closet paranormal enthusiast in debunker's clothing. He needed to play the debunker in order to avoid being kicked out of the science club while exploring subjects like UFOs and interstellar contact (as in his novel *Contact*, Sagan, 1997B).

Now for some of the basics. Ian Stevenson (1997B: 1, 5) found that one in 500 children surveyed in northern India claimed to remember a past life. He thought that such a relatively high incidence might be explained by the fact that there is less rebuke of children showing such tendencies in cultures like India in which there is widespread acceptance of reincarnation. I might add parenthetically that I have heard families with New Age beliefs in the U.S. talk about their young children giving indications of past lives, or telling about how they themselves had such memories when children. Stevenson says that children who remember past lives speak about them with emotion between the ages of about 2 and 4, then typically forget them.

Stevenson (1997B: 7) reports that 35% of such children have phobias, often linked to their past-life experiences. High percentages, in various samples in different countries, 51%, 29%, and 74%, recall having had violent deaths (Stevenson, 1997B: 8). Tucker's (2005:214) sample of cases shows 70% reporting an unnatural death. These findings connect to the theme of emotions causing paranormal connections, as in hauntings, or crisis apparitions, or ESP warnings in family emergencies. In this case the idea would be that, however many people might have had past lives, they would be more likely to remember them if they had died a violent death, due to the emotional trauma.

Leo Sprinkle, UFO researcher and counselor, told me that his first two cases of people reporting past lives to him came unexpectedly when he asked them to recall their first memory of a traumatic event, e.g. involving a fear of dogs. He hadn't asked them about past lives, but they reported spontaneously events like having been killed by a pack of dogs.

According to Stevenson (1997B: 9) there are four nearly universal aspects involved in children's past-life memories: speaking about them at an early age, later on stopping speaking about them, a high percentage of recalling violent deaths, and mentioning the mode of death.

Now for the critique. Gauld (1982: 172) points out that Stevenson, appropriately skeptical about his own work, provides his critics with ammunition for attacking him by suggesting alternative explanations. First let's consider normal alternative explanations for reports of past lives. People have faulty memories (of what young children did or said that might indicate past lives), relatives and friends may influence the children's behavior in a culture conducive to belief in reincarnation, and there may be intentional fraud (Tucker, 2005: ix).

There is also the theoretical objection that if there were reincarnation, it would be unable to provide enough souls for the population explosion (Tucker, 2005: 198-199). However, this assumption overlooks possible scenarios in which there are a great many souls who never incarnate, perhaps not everyone has had a past life, new souls can be created, old souls divide to become many, or the length of time between reincarnations becomes shorter as the population grows. Obviously the speculation exceeds our knowledge, on both sides of the debate.

Stevenson (1997B: 9-11) was well aware of the methodological difficulties involved in eliminating normal explanations. He interviewed both present and past-life families (the survivors), and collected documents and photos. Some of his defenses against error included comparing testimonies and looking for comparable features in very different cultures. Only a small percentage of cases could be recorded from the very beginning, before others could influence the children. However, he noticed that parents often hesitated identifying their children as having had a past life, and he thought that contaminating encouragement was seldom a significant factor.

Aside from normal explanations, there are also alternative paranormal explanations to consider. These include ESP (tuning in on the life of somebody in the past), and possession (of the living person by the spirit of the deceased "past-life" person) (Tucker, 2005: 45-46; Becker, 1993: 11-13). Stevenson (1997B: 11) countered by saying that the children rarely showed the ability to perform ESP of this kind and that their memories typically faded, which would make the possession seem less likely.

Nevertheless, Stevenson (1997B: 2) recognized that all of these criticisms were troubling and difficult to dismiss. Only one percent of the 2,600 cases investigated by his team could be recorded from the very beginning, before anyone else in the social environment had begun to label the case as reincarnation. He recognized the possibilities of mingled memories and of giving the child more credit than appropriate for behaving mysteriously.

For these reasons, Stevenson considered the biological evidence he collected of birthmarks in children that matched fatal wounds or other marks on the deceased to be superior to the interview evidence. The birthmarks were not the usual moles, but "hairless areas of puckered, scarlike tissue, often raised above surrounding tissues or depressed below them" (Stevenson, 1997B: 3). These might represent, for example, the entrance and exit wounds of a bullet that had killed the person identified in the past life, and could be verified in the death records. He concluded, "Despite the obvious difficulties that the concept of reincarnation poses . . . for modern science . . . , the birthmarks and birth defects in these cases do not lend themselves easily to explanations other than reincarnation" (Stevenson, 1997B: 2).

Keep in mind that Stevenson thought that the evidence was consistent with the concept of reincarnation. We are still left with the mystery of what might survive in reincarnation and how it might work. Stevenson (1997B: 181-184; cf. also Tucker, 2005: 215-223) thought that discarnate personalities between lives might be like dreams, NDEs etc., and that they might take the form of a kind of template that would then affect the features of a developing embryo. The personality, he thought, might choose its new parents, something that seems to happen even before death, as in the case of "announcing."

Announcing dreams are especially noted among the Tlingit (Native Americans of the Northwest Coast) and Burmese (Stevenson, 1997B: 3-4). For example, an elder dreams of being reincarnated as his grandson and tells other relatives about it, and they later notice that the young grandson acts as if he is the grandfather and can identify objects that belonged to him. This recalls the pattern in Tibetan Buddhism of trying to find the reincarnated dalai lama through finding a child who remembers the past life and can identify objects belonging to the previous dalai lama.

Not surprisingly, Becker (1993: 36) states that we need evidence on the nature of the disembodied state between reincarnations. That would be nice.

For those who would like to explore Ian Stevenson's life and work in greater depth, I highly recommend the issue of the *Journal of Scientific Exploration*, V. 22, #1, 2008, that is dedicated entirely to this subject.

From my perspective, reincarnation is a fascinating subject to explore for evidence of survival. To begin with, for most of my life I had never embraced it, thinking it likely to be a religious fantasy. I first had second thoughts about it when I participated in a past-life recall exercise in the 1970s. We were asked to imagine going up in a hot-air balloon and coming down in another place and time on earth. The detailed imagery I got surprised me, and I had the notion that I was in a tiny town near the border of Germany and Italy. Later on I looked up the odd name on a detailed map and found it. I was astonished that it was there, right were I thought it would be. Of course this could be some kind of ESP or even cryptomnesia, if I had remembered subconsciously a detailed map I had seen in the past but had forgotten on a conscious level.

Years later, in the 1980s, I read some of the work of Ian Stevenson and others on reincarnation and thought that the evidence was well worth considering. Then in 1995 I attended a UFO conference in Laramie,

Wyoming, at which Leo Sprinkle offered to do a past-life reading on me. I found it very amusing, but I didn't give what he told me a lot of credence. On the way back to my motel room I walked around the entire building, reminiscing about my experiences there the previous year when I had attended the same conference. That delayed me just enough so that when I walked into my room and turned on the TV (to a channel I had not selected), the very first thing I heard from the set was, "Welcome to the Past-Life Pavilion," a line from the film "Defending Your Life." This synchronicity gave me pause, as if the universe might be trying to tell me to pay attention to the idea of past lives, or to bring it below my threshold of eye-rolling, an idea I learned from Leo Sprinkle.

Fast forward to the early 2000s. Penelope and I sat at a table in Chautauqua, New York, at a book signing for us (*Guided by Spirit*, 2003) and two other authors. One of the other authors was a member of the same department in the Medical School at University of Virginia that Ian Stevenson belonged to. I asked him what his colleagues thought of Stevenson, and he told me that he was not respected because he studied reincarnation. I found this ironic, considering that Stevenson was such a careful guy. He talked about "cases suggestive of reincarnation."

And on one occasion I saw Stevenson at the banquet for the Society for Scientific Exploration, to which he and I both belonged. The person sitting beside me pointed Stevenson out and told me that he had wanted to introduce him to another person who did research on reincarnation, but that Stevenson had declined on the grounds that he didn't think that the other person was careful enough in his methodology.

All of this makes sense in terms of the sociology of science. Reincarnation is a taboo subject in normal science, and it makes no difference what you say about it or how careful you are in your methodology. Under such circumstances, or taking them into consideration, can we extract ourselves from the constraining frames of normal science and religion and learn something about the possibility of survival from the data?

PENELOPE'S COMMENTS:

When we conducted interviews for this book the scientists were looking outside of themselves and reporting on what they observed. Charlie asked me to give an insider's point of view as a mystic. I appeared to procrastinate on doing so for months. Finally I recognized that I was reluctant to put myself out there with people (readers) I did not know. I had a sense of privacy about my life. It is one thing to write about what I have researched (other people's experiences), another to share visions and emotions intensely felt by myself. I learned very young that sharing a past life or vision, or doing mediumship was treated respectfully at my grandmother's house, but it set myself up for ridicule with my parents or others in the world.

In my personal experience reincarnation has always been a fact, rather like hearing and believing that the earth is round or knowing about the law of gravity. But just as I rarely think about that, I probably think of a past life only once or twice a year. To me the only purpose of remembering a past life is to notice what talents, interests or lessons from then could be useful or expressed today. Or we can discover a process today that would heal both the past-life experience and the present, helping us to evolve into an equanimous, loving state of consciousness.

That said, when I have felt the opposite of equanimous, that is intensely emotional, such as mad, sad, hurt or fearful, I check out first what value of mine has been violated. Then what from my past, this time around, am I being given a chance to heal? Usually I find the answer. If not, I will ask to recall another time or place and think about how it relates to today.

A good example occurred when Charlie and I visited Natural Bridge in Virginia. We were having a pleasant drive on Route 81 in Virginia when we decided to stop for a break as we saw signs for Natural Bridge, which I had never heard of. It was a commercial place, but we paid and took an elevator down to a ravine. I was curious and happy as I walked down the path ahead until I saw the natural bridge rock formation over the creek. Without warning I started to cry. Charlie rushed up to me, thinking I was physically hurt, as I'm not a person who cries very often. We stepped off the path; I was drawing attention from others. I sobbed out, "I never thought I would see it again!" My soul longed to be here again; I have never experienced such homesickness. I immediately felt fine again and savored each step along the walk. It was such a treat to be there.

Afterward we learned that Thomas Jefferson had owned it. I had already had many experiences of recollection of the time I was a male friend of Jefferson. Standing for the first time at Independence Hall in Philadelphia the park ranger had said to us tourists, "This room is an exact replica of the way it was when the Declaration of Independence was signed." Somehow I knew that wasn't so, so I raised my hand and asked her about the pediments above the doors across the room. She ushered Charlie and me to the hallway and began asking questions. I knew better than to appear a "loony" by saying that I had been there in 1776 and the turnings over the door had not. I gave some answer that satisfied her, and then she said, "We just had those installed before a Chinese delegation arrives." The purpose of the pediments was to obscure new security cameras, and the public was not supposed to know about them.

I had similar experiences when touring Monticello the first time and knowing what was the same and what had changed. It was like watching a film of what was then projected over how it appeared to my eyes today. Watching a waking vision.

Some years later while Charlie was filming an interview for this book at The Monroe Institute, I decided to take a drive over to Monticello. Approaching it, I heard a direct voice (it seemed to be outside my head) say, "Stop here!" So I pulled over and parked the car. I cannot say if I was acting as a medium for a man from the 1700s or recalling myself from that time. I knew I was eager to walk over through a field. I knew exactly where my destination was and headed for that spot. When I got there in about ten minutes I sat down with a contented sigh. Then I smelled wild strawberries, looked down closely and could see that I was surrounded by them. In fact I had stained my pants by sitting on some. I was delighted that they were still growing there after more than 200 years.

So this kind of experience has always been commonplace for me, but often no big deal, just pleasant memories. I have never known my name from those lives, never been a famous person. I have been male and female, young and old, of many temperaments and from many places.

PART FOUR

MAKING SOMETHING OF IT

Chapter Seventeen

PRACTICAL APPLICATIONS

Harking back to the Introduction, you'll recall that the purpose of this book was to satisfy curiosity about consciousness and what happens to it after we die. The sociology of science perspective makes it possible to see how different "frames" result in different attitudes about the evidence, or even about whether there could be such a thing as evidence for consciousness and for life after death. We didn't really claim to be looking for practical applications for knowledge about consciousness.

Nevertheless, during the course of the research we occasionally ran into the frame that practicality was what counted. This should really be no surprise. As a sociologist of religion, I am well aware that religions typically don't ask scientific questions about life after death (Spiritualism is an exception). They usually make it a matter of faith or belief. Sometimes they argue about whether these beliefs are good for you, or contribute to good physical and mental health (which is a question that sociologists of religion sometimes ask as well).

In spite of our focus on the question of scientific evidence, some of our interviews and participant observation revealed either anti-scientific attitudes (e.g., "Let's leave the scientists out of this!") or the attitude that experience is primary, and that so-called objective scientific evidence is either not necessary or not easy to get, especially considering the opposition to such research in normal, mainstream science.

In spite of my curiosity addiction, which really wants to know, not just believe or pretend, I need to respect these frames and see their usefulness. Therefore, we need to say a little something in this chapter about practical applications both of the scientific evidence about so-called paranormal consciousness, such as it is, and of the assumptions that paranormal consciousness exists (evidence or no evidence).

For one thing, sometimes paranormal researchers claim that their evidence helps people reduce their fear of death, especially in the cases of reincarnation, spirit mediumship, and NDEs. Alan Gauld (2008: 32) stated that Ian Stevenson thought that belief in reincarnation would reduce people's fear of death. This makes sense in terms of Ernest Becker's (1973) denial of death theory, in which religion is seen as a product of human ability to foresee death and be anxious about it.

Gary Schwartz (2002) considers at length the social consequences of being able to prove scientifically, through studies of spirit mediums, that we can communicate with the spirits of the dead. These consequences include not only less fear of death, but also less competitiveness to accomplish everything before dying, using spirit mediums as witnesses in murder cases to bring in testimony from murder victims, and helping survivors with grief reduction.

Recall also that in Chapter Ten we referred to the finding that a high percentage of people who experience NDEs come back with less fear of death. Moreover, they sometimes exhibit a radical change in personality; whether this transformation is "good" or not might be difficult to judge.

Lucid dreaming is another phenomenon with potential practical applications. Stephen LaBerge (1985, 2-3) stated that LD has "potential for promoting personal growth, self-development, enhancing self-confidence, improving mental and physical health, facilitating creative problem solving, and helping you to progress on the path to self-mastery." Robert Waggoner (2009: 155-156) discusses the process of healing oneself in lucid dreams, much as one can be healed under hypnosis.

Undoubtedly the most significant example we encountered of using consciousness for health and self-development is The Monroe Institute (TMI) in Virginia. See Ronald Russell's book *The Journey of Robert Monroe: From Out-of-Body Explorer to Consciousness Pioneer* (2007), especially Chapter 13, "Robert Monroe and the Exploration of Consciousness" at TMI.

When we interviewed people on the staff at TMI, Paul Rademacher, the director, told us about the history of Robert Monroe's work with sound (as with their Hemi-Synch technology) and resultant levels of consciousness in their laboratories, and showed us the facilities to which people come for workshops. Frederick (Skip) Atwater, discussed the importance of experiencing phenomena like remote viewing. Darlene Miller and Patty Ray Avalon gave the testimonials of themselves and others about the benefits of their Gateway Program and numerous other graduate programs for various types of development. Monroe was known for his own OBEs, but TMI deals with a wide variety of psychic/spiritual exploration, letting people have their own experiences without labeling them.

Science is important at TMI, but it is applied science for the most part, recording data to help refine the experience. Cam Danielson in 2008 did an evaluation of TMI's programs for them, in which it was found that a high percentage of participants had peak psychological experiences as a result of their workshops.

Perhaps the best known TMI testimonial comes from Maureen Caudill (2006: 2-25) in her book *Suddenly Psychic: A Skeptic's Journey*. She went to TMI after some personal crises, and found herself a "techie nerd" in a room full of New Agers, taking the Gateway Program. At first she was very skeptical, but she found that she could bring through spirit messages, do remote viewing, and heal her desperately ill cat at a distance of 2,500 miles. Having taken a big psychic leap in six days (thus the title *Suddenly Psychic*), she couldn't accept the world in "simple scientific terms" any longer, and she had to reconcile her strange experiences with science.

She also gives a good explanation of TMI and their Hemi-Synch technology (Caudill, 2006: 13-25). See also our DVD Documentary, "Science and Spirit(s)" (Emmons and Emmons, 2011) for interviews with the above-mentioned TMI staff and for views of the grounds.

Some other examples of practical applications of "mysterious" consciousness can be found in Simon (2008: 349-402), *Measuring the Immeasurable: The Scientific Case for Spirituality*, especially in regard to health through yoga, meditation, prayer and distance healing. Some of these practices, such as yoga and meditation, used to be considered paranormal, but they are beginning to move from alternative into "normal" medicine because of the obvious health benefits. My view is that the paranormal becomes normal just as soon as it can be shown to make money legitimately in a capitalist system.

Our last previous research on the New Spirituality (or New Age) Movement considers the way it blends science and religion/spirituality into a combined treatment of body, mind and spirit. In spite of legitimating itself to a great extent with scientific explanations (such as quantum physics), much of the culture content in this movement is also antiscience or at least not very scientifically rigorous (as with most religions). The general attitude is that you should take up whatever beliefs and practices suit you. Thus the title of our DVD documentary, "Roll Your Own Religion: New Spirituality in North America" (Emmons and Emmons, 2010).

Returning to the main focus of this book, the issue of whether there is scientific evidence for consciousness apart from the body or for the survival of consciousness after death, the main obstacle to research on these questions is normal science. Nevertheless, there are scientists and others who explore these questions with little or no research funding. This book focuses on what we might know about consciousness from the existing research, most of which is not mainstream, except for the part on neuroscience, for example. Imagine what we might learn in the future, if practical concerns, such as medical applications, legitimate much greater funding for such research.

PENELOPE'S COMMENTS:

In my own experience there is a nonlocal entanglement where all information that I need can be accessed, simply known. I think we can all know anything without ever knowing why. So, I have chosen to practice this in my life.

On a mundane level: shopping. I rarely shop on impulse. I keep a running list of what I want or need. Then, like yesterday when I was parking at a pharmacy to pick up Vitamin B, I looked over at another store and knew they had the winter coat I wanted. I had given away a twenty-year-old red wool coat last fall and thought I would replace it someday. I walked into the department store and saw it in my size, on sale 60% off. When I got to the counter the sales woman gave me a coupon for another 40 % percent off, so this lovely red wool coat cost me under $60.00 and less than ten minutes of time.

I could tell stories of hundreds of experiences over the years that have shown me that there is no need to search and shop for things. I just decide what I want, write it down to tell the universe, not care a lot if or when it happens (nonattachment to the outcome), and then I know (clairvoyance?) and receive them at the right place, right time, right price. Because I have the habit of releasing something from my closet when I bring in a new item, deciding what to get rid of has been more difficult than the purchase!

We can know other practical things, just by our gut knowing, our dreams, our feelings that say, "Yes, let's do it!", or "No, I don't want that now." When Charlie and I were living separately in Erie, and going to rent a house together in Gettysburg, he asked me for a month to commit to traveling there and looking at housing. I appeared to both of us to be procrastinating; I just did not want to go. Then I had a dream and felt that I finally wanted to go there, so we drove to Gettysburg. That morning a house had been listed in the college provost's office (only), and we rented it. It came with a delightful landlady who suggested we choose new paint and carpet. It would not have been known to us if we had gone before that day.

Chapter Eighteen

SUMMING UP AND LOOKING TO THE FUTURE

Another point we made in the introduction was that we were not going to attempt to give a detailed evaluation of the evidence for all of the subtopics referred to in this book. Instead we have summed up the main types of evidence, problematic points, and kinds of frames within which scientists and others examine (or refuse to examine) the evidence. We have also pointed out some major sources you can check for further reading.

Even if we had made this book ten times as long, I don't think that an encyclopedic review of the evidence would have solved the central issues. As a sociologist, I think I can make a contribution by pointing out the different "frames" that researchers in different disciplines, different normal or alternative scientific communities, etc., use for looking at these questions.

Without this concept of frames, it might seem inexplicable how two different scientists could see the same evidence so differently. How could behavioral psychologists have denied the existence of consciousness at one time? Why are neuroscientists looking for it now? Why is the chess game played between Korchnoi and (allegedly) Moroczy, with the help of a spirit medium, considered by Russell Targ to be the "gold standard" for evidence for survival; but the same game is considered "not impressive" by one social scientist I interviewed? The answer, I think, can be found in the scientific frames or paradigms they are using, and in the academic or scientific communities they belong to, as much as to personal whims or biases. Sometimes these factors are difficult to sort out, but at least it is clear that the evidence does not speak the same way to all. There are social as well as psychological processes involved. Such evidence is not simply evaluated by an automatic process of "objective science."

One of the major disagreements over frames can be found in the use of quantum physics. Whereas many of the so-called "paranormal" phenomena considered here, such as ESP or remote viewing, OBEs/ NDEs, and psychic healing, seem impossible in Newtonian physics, they might make sense in quantum physics because of the concept of entanglement or nonlocal connections. Researchers like Dean Radin and Robert Jahn in laboratory parapsychology want to apply the quantum physics frame, even though it is not possible to demonstrate the precise mechanisms involved. Using quantum physics on the level of large-scale phenomena, instead of just the tiny, quantum level, however, is not yet generally acceptable in psychology or neuroscience. Just the same, there are also tiny subparts within the brain, for example, that could be subject to quantum-level phenomena.

Another framing issue involves acceptable methodology for subjective experiences, especially those involving consciousness. As noted before, behavioral psychologists claimed that consciousness was either nonexistent or nonresearchable, because subjective statements about one's own consciousness were not considered objectively scientific. Since the 1990s, however, there has been considerable interest in consciousness in psychology, because it has become closely allied with neuroscience in biology.

Neuroscientists have a new technology and methodology for looking into the brain, previously considered a mysterious "black box" by the behavioral psychologists. The fact that they cannot find the location of consciousness in the brain, but can merely see what "lights up" when we think about different things, suggests that subjective experience may actually be an important source for information about consciousness. Bringing the objective neuroscientific methodology together with subjective reports in psychology and sociology might be fruitful, as many have suggested.

Scientists who are stuck in the frame that considers all consciousness to be contained within the skull of a living person, no matter what the evidence from the parapsychological, quantum physical perspective seems to indicate, tend to reject out of hand the possibilities for ESP, OBEs/NDEs, PK, and healing at a distance. Parapsychologists and others who do consider such evidence, are still stymied when it comes to locating exact mechanisms by which these things might occur. Perhaps a living brain is necessary for psi to occur, as Radin says. If so, then parapsychologists need to take on the frame of neuroscience as well (which some do). As I tell my students in sociological methods class, multiple methodologies (and frames in general) are very useful for getting an integrated picture.

The next major framing issue occurs within parapsychology itself. It involves the super-ESP frame and the survival frame. Consciousness apart from the brain is easier to accept in the quantum physics frame (or super-ESP frame) than is the survival of consciousness after death, which seems to some to require a religious/spiritual frame. Wait, you say, why not just look at the evidence, and see which frame or frames (theory or theories, in this case) would be supported by the data? Indeed.

Because of the fact that we have even less of an idea how survival might work, compared to ESP, which might be a normal quantum-mechanical function, we tend to jump to the conclusion that survival (as evidenced perhaps by spirit mediumship, ghosts, NDEs, and reincarnation) requires a supernatural or religious/spiritual frame. And of course, this is where normal scientists would get off the boat. Therefore, parapsychologists tend to shy away from survival as an explanation for such phenomena as spirit mediumship, and prefer (super)-ESP, which can be more easily seen in a scientific frame (with quantum physics).

This would lead us into a kind of dualism: natural vs. supernatural (or physical vs. spiritual). Operating on speculation alone, admittedly, we might frame this differently and imagine that what we now consider spiritual is really natural rather than supernatural; eventually we may discover that the "spirit world" is continuous with the rest of nature. This would mean that life after death might have an explanation within the scientific frame. We just don't understand what it is right now.

Because of the fact that we have so little idea of what a surviving consciousness might be like, it is difficult to know what it is that survives, if anything. One method is just to speculate that it might include memory, personality, the ability to play chess (mentally), etc. Another method is just to see what evidence there is for what survives, based on the content of the subjective experiences involved in NDEs, apparitions, spirit mediums' messages, and past-life recall, especially in cases that are evidential (collective cases with multiple witnesses and/or paranormal info).

Looking into the future, what further developments might there be in the "scientific search for spirit" (an early title we considered for this book)? It is tempting to hope for advancements in physical science that may explain better the hidden order involved in the quantum world, or in multiple dimensions etc. This is beyond most of us to imagine, but it is a possibility frequently mentioned.

Not everybody agrees with this, however. Stephen Braude, for example, a philosophy professor, told me in an interview that he thought that the emphasis on quantum physics in parapsychology was misguided. He thought that it was a reductionist tendency to see everything in terms of physics and laboratory methodology, due to excessive attachment to its prestige. He would rather see greater emphasis on the collection and thorough analysis of spontaneous cases and large-scale phenomena (as in the case of PK), using psychological and sociological methodologies, since these occurrences are indeed found within a psychosocial context.

Aside from the methodologies used, there is of course the larger question of whether normal, mainstream science is likely to pay more attention in the future to consciousness studies and to fund some of these alternate frames or disciplines, like parapsychology. In 1984, James McClenon (*Deviant Science: The Case of Parapsychology*: 221-235) wrote about how science still rejected the study of psi anomalies, but that it might not always, depending on changes in the general culture away from materialism and toward consciousness. In his interview with me in 2010, however, he did not see much future for parapsychology as a discipline.

By 1997 Dean Radin (1997, 2-5, 264, 303), however, already thought that there were shifting opinions in the scientific community, that scientific journals were becoming more favorable toward psi research, and that interest in consciousness was on the increase. He also predicted increased investment by corporations. In 2008 I was told in an interview by someone who should know that a Portuguese pharmaceutical company had tried to endow a chair in parapsychological research at a major university in the UK. I can only imagine that the motivation for this was that alternative medical treatments involving, for example, healing intentions at a distance, can be researched in the laboratory (as they are at IONS in California). In 2007 (166-169), Beauregard and O'Leary also talked about a shift to more serious consideration of psi research.

I can think of two other institutions, other than science, medicine, and business, in which there have been signs of acceptance of psi research. One is the CIA with its studies of remote viewing (Targ and Katra, 1998). The other is law enforcement with their sometime use of psychics and spirit mediums in detective work. Laine Crosby, who identifies herself as a psychic investigator and spirit medium, told me in an interview that she is used in many police investigations because her work has been legitimated by an individual who organizes searches in missing-person cases and has experienced the effectiveness of her work.

THE BOTTOM LINES (What We Think)

Charlie:

It is not possible to have gotten this far in the book without having revealed our own attitudes to some degree. Although I try to be fair, I doubt that anybody can ever be "objective" in science, including social science. I have already said that my major frames for looking at the subject of this book are sociology and Spiritualism. Also, I have a curiosity addiction, which means that I really want to know what's going on, rather than tricking myself into believing something comfortable or interesting.

The next thing I should say is that the only thing I know for sure is that I don't know anything for sure. (Socrates said that the only think that he knew was that he knew nothing. However, I'm not that sure of myself. I might actually know something and not realize it.) This is one of the core principles in science in general and in sociology in particular. The true spirit or ethos of science is open-minded inquiry, not the locking up of "truth" in a box. And Peter Berger (*Invitation to Sociology*, 1963) wrote, "Things may not be what they seem."

So, how do things seem to me, and how do I imagine that I might know? Throughout my life I have had lots of apparently paranormal experiences, not before the age of 19, but beginning with the course I took in psychology in college that dealt in part with ESP and PK, and especially in the mid-1990s when I had a kind of spiritual awakening. I doubt that I would have changed from being an atheist or agnostic, or a believer in a materialist explanation of the universe if I had not had those experiences. There's nothing like an experience.

Having said that, I still look for evidence. It's just that I also consider my own experiences to be evidence, not just what I read about or collect myself as data from other people. And, again, I always imagine that what I think could be wrong. Sociology is a very subversive discipline, questioning or deconstructing standard views of reality; but you can't be a real sociologist without deconstructing yourself and your own beliefs as well.

Now, it's difficult for me not to accept ESP, not just because I have read a lot of evidence for it in the literature, but also because of lots of personal experiences that seem hard to explain any other way. One example would be the time Penelope reached for the duct tape and put it on the counter for no reason, apparently having no idea that I needed it. Any one such example would not be sufficient, but there are so many.

The same goes for spirit mediumship which I have studied both in library research and from participant observation (Emmons and Emmons, 2003). Likewise for apparitions, PK, and spiritual healing.

So far I am just saying that I think that there is something very interesting going on with all of these phenomena. And they seem to be paranormal, at least in the really good cases, although I would not stake that judgment on any one particular case, which might be flawed. As far as super cases go, I think that I agree with Russell Targ that the chess game is the gold standard, not only for indicating something paranormal, but for suggesting a survival explanation. Could I be wrong about that? Could there be a normal explanation for the chess game? I think it's possible; I can't be 100% sure. A paranormal explanation that avoids survival might be that the medium used telepathy to pick up what Korchnoi (the living chess player) expected Maroczy's next move to be.

Nevertheless, in general I would say that my level of acceptance of these phenomena is high enough to think that they deserve serious study funded with serious money. That is really all one needs to legitimate scientific attention to a topic. As my UFO researchers said, it's not a question of belief. It's a matter of evidence.

I also think that psi is an important subject. If there really are such phenomena, the very fact that they defy our standard paradigms (frames), except maybe for quantum physics, indicates that we may not understand very well the fundamental structure of reality.

Everything I have said so far is, I think, the most important to be said. I don't know anything for sure. Evidence seems to suggest that psi phenomena are real, though unexplained. They deserve serious research.

Now to go out on a limb, here's what I suppose to be going on. The universe is all one thing, interconnected or entangled. Some things and consciousnesses are more entangled than others, or can make use of the entanglement more easily due to emotional connections or other such ties.

Next, our subjective experience of consciousness (I'm taking the leap of assuming that your consciousness is basically like mine, although I can never know that you or anything else is not a mere illusion created in my mind) proves that we exist in some real sense. However, we don't know everything about the differences among levels of awakeness, as in the case of regular dreams vs. lucid dreams vs. what we call "awake." Maybe there is some more awake state in which we will all get the joke.

Although I am more certain about consciousness extending beyond the brain (at least by entanglement if not actually "physically"), I also think that there is probably survival of consciousness after "so-called death," as we Spiritualists call it. Probably the main reasons I think this are my experiences with spirit mediumship (including observing Penelope, as well as observing myself as a medium), the chess game case (Maroczy vs. Korchnoi), and the evidence for reincarnation, especially the birth marks. NDEs and apparitions are interesting, but it is easier for me to think of nonsurvival explanations for these experiences, at least in most cases.

What I find it really difficult to form an opinion about is why. Why should we, or anything at all, exist? At this point I'm into philosophical speculation, which I suppose to be more a product of what I would like to be than a reasonable guess as to what is. I truly think that it is beyond me, and perhaps beyond all humans to imagine. This doesn't stop people from imagining, or from claiming they know based on religious faith or channeling deities and other intelligences.

I think that the most interesting way of putting the question here is the one attributed to Einstein: "Is the Universe a friendly place?" This reminds me of the logic I used when I was an atheist. "Why should I pretend to believe in God if I don't? I think that if there is a God, she/he/it will give me credit for being honest about my lack of belief."

At this point I am a Spiritualist, because Spiritualists are (in theory) allowed to decide to believe anything they want. Technically I am still an atheist or agnostic, because I have no concept of a separate super-being with a personality. I could easily be wrong about that of course.

My spiritual insight that I imagine receiving from my deceased relatives tells me to do the following: 1. don't worry too much, 2. radiate love, and 3. count your blessings. Many New Agers, of which I guess I am one, emphasize that everything is Love. Or they will say, "God the good is all there is."

The sociologist of religion in me steps back and sees this as another example of the denial of death theory of religion. One of my interviewees, a sociologist, told me that the question of survival is unanswerable, and the important thing is to understand why we ask this question. We ask it because we want to know whether we are going to survive (each of us separately, not whether survival happens in general).

So, to complete the sociological deconstruction of myself, not to mention others, perhaps the real reason I am curious about the subject of this book is not really my curiosity addiction, but rather a vested interest in cheating death. Be that as it may, I still think it was fun to do this. And one more thing: the rebel in me likes to challenge the smuggies in mainstream academe who make the rules about what questions should be asked in science. Science should always ask questions about everything.

Penelope:

As we dived into what various disciplines of science say about topics like mediumship, NDEs and reincarnation, I recognized that for myself I wanted to spend my time on earth in my seventh decade serving others, going to the still, small voice within, and observing what the life lessons of an elder hold for me and others. I chose to participate in the interviews and to read Charlie's view of their view (frame). However, he wanted more of me, an experiencer's frame of reference, point of view from the inside, rather than observing the outside manifestation.

Carl Jung said that religion is a system designed to keep us from the experience of God. I would amend that by exchanging the word Love for the word God. The various disciplines of science appear to encourage a limiting, instead of all-encompassing viewpoint, or frame, of experiencing and measuring life in a physical body. Nonphysical consciousness is not measureable, so many people do not think it exists, or they place people's nonmeasurable experiences under the heading of deviance.

I am disenchanted by people who would say in effect, "There is no such thing as consciousness." (It can't be measured; therefore it doesn't exist). I think that is denial or dogma instead of curiosity. At the same time, others appear to me like the blind men describing the elephant: each man would describe one part, such as the elephant's head, or tail or side. Wouldn't it be wonderful if all of us could combine our viewpoints into a gestalt? I recognize that my consciousness is "odd" because I can hear discarnate beings, and see nonphysical realities and visions from the so-called past, present or future. I say "so-called" because in my perception of the universe the now moment contains everything. Time is an illusion. Sometimes I have noticed that people's egos are invested in the academic stance of being right and proving their point, all of the ego's one-up-man-ship and competition nurtured by our educational system. I view Charlie's comprehensive social scientist's willingness to consider all frames as exceptional. I think the readers of this book will also.

Reading Charlie's part of this book, I can be hopeful that seeing the varied viewpoints (frames) will enlarge our human conception of what is possible. The idea of being right is a byproduct of our culture and has little to do with our identity as Spirit, the fact that we are one drop in the whole ocean of life. Yet each consciousness adds to the whole, and just by the fact that we are he, we are necessary and integral parts of the whole. It wouldn't be an ocean without the drops in the bucket. I am hopeful that this book will help us move from dualism to a more encompassing paradigm and to an evolving human consciousness.

Bibliography

Aronowitz, Stanley

    1988 *Science As Power*. Minneapolis: University of Minnesota.

Atwater, P.M.H.

    2007 *The Big Book of Near-Death Experiences*. Charlottesville, VA: Hampton Roads Pub. Co.

Beauregard, Mario and Denyse O'Leary

    2007 *The Spiritual Brain: A Neuroscientist's Case for the Existence of the Soul*. NY: HarperOne.

Becker, Carl B.

    1993 *Paranormal Experience and Survival of Death*. Albany, NY: SUNY Press.

Becker, Ernest

    1973 *The Denial of Death*. NY: Simon $ Schuster.

Benson, Herbert and Miriam Z. Klipper

    2000 *The Relaxation Response*. NY: Wm. Morrow.

Berger, Peter

    1963 *Invitation to Sociology: A Humanistic Perspective*. NY: Anchor.

Blackmore, Susan

    2005 *Consciousness: A Very Short Introduction*. NY: Oxford U. Press.

    2006 *Conversations on Consciousness*. NY: Oxford U. Press.

Blum, Deborah

    2006 *Ghost Hunters: William James and the Search for Scientific Proof for Life After Death*. NY: Penguin Press.

Boes, Roderick H.

    2009 *The Physics of Encounter: Toward a Theory of Consciousness*. Victoria, Canada: Trafford Pub.

Braude, Stephen

> 1997 *The Limits of Influence: Psychokinesis and the Philosophy of Science*. Lanham, MD: University Press of America.
>
> 2003 *Immortal Remains: The Evidence for Life after Death*. Lanham, MD: Rowman & Littlefield Pub., Inc.
>
> 2007 *The Gold Leaf Lady and Other Parapsychological Investigations*. Chicago: U of Chicago Press.

Carter, Rita

> 2002 *Exploring Consciousness*. Berkeley: U of California Press.

Caudill, Maureen

> 2006 *Suddenly Psychic: A Skeptic's Journey*. Charlottesville, VA: Hampton Roads.

Chalmers, David

> 2007 "The Hard Problem of Consciousness", pp. 225-235 in Velmans and Schneider (eds.): *The Blackwell Companion to Consciousness*. Malden, MA: Blackwell Pub.

Crick, Francis

> 1994 *The Astonishing Hypothesis: The Scientific Search for the Soul*. NY: Charles Scribner's Sons.

Edwards, Paul

> 2002 *Reincarnation: A Critical Examination*. Amherst, NY: Prometheus Books.

Eisenbeiss, Wolfgang, and Dieter Hassler

> 2006 "An Assessment of Ostensible Communications with a Deceased Grandmaster as Evidence for Survival," *Journal of the Society for Psychical Research*, 70.2, 883, April, pp. 65-97.

Emmons, Charles F.

> 1982 *Chinese Ghosts and ESP: A Study of Paranormal Beliefs and Experiences*. Metuchen, New Jersey: The Scarecrow Press, Inc.
>
> 1997 *At the Threshold: UFOs, Science and the New Age*. Mill Spring, North Carolina: Wild Flower Press.

Emmons, Charles F. and Penelope Emmons

2003 *Guided by Spirit: A Journey into the Mind of the Medium*. NY: Writers Club Press.

2010 "Roll Your Own Religion: New Spirituality in North America," documentary DVD.

2011 "Science and Spirit(s)," documentary DVD.

Evans, Hilary

2002 *Seeing Ghosts: Experiences of the Paranormal*. London: John Murray.

Fontana, David

2003 *Psychology, Religion, and Spirituality*. Malden, MA: BPS Blackwell.

Fox, Mark

2003 *Religion, Spirituality and the Near-Death Experience*. London: Routledge.

Gazzaniga, Michael S.

2008 *Human: The Science Behind What Makes Us Unique*. NY: Harper Collins.

Gauld, Alan

1982 *Mediumship and Survival: A Century of Investigations*. London: Heinemann.

Goffman, Erving

1974 *Frame Analysis: An Essay on the Organization of Experience*. NY: Harper Colophon Books.

Greeley, Andrew M.

1991 "The Paranormal Is Normal," *Journal of the American Society for Psychical Research*, 85, pp. 367-374.

Greyson, Bruce

2008 "Ian Stevenson's Contributions to Near-Death Studies," *Journal of Scientific Exploration*, 22, 1, pp. 54-63.

Grossman, Neal and David Schaffer Hafiz

2010 Review of Charles T. Tart, *The End of Materialism, Journal of Scientific Exploration*, 24, 1, pp. 109-158.

Grosso, Michael

2008 "Hume's Syndrome: Irrational Resistance to the Paranormal," *Journal of Scientific Exploration*, 22, 4, pp. 549-556.

Heath, Pamela Rae
2000 "The PK Zone: A Phenomenological Study," *The Journal of Parapsychology*, 64, March, pp. 53-72.

Horgan, John
1999 *The Undiscovered Mind: How the Human Brain Defies Replication, Medication, and Explanation.* NY: The Free Press.
2003 *Rational Mysticism: Dispatches from the Border Between Science and Spirituality.* NY: Houghton Mifflin Co.

Jacobson, Nils O.
1974 *Life Without Death?: On Parapsychology, Mysticism, and the Question of Survival.* U.S.: Delacorte Press.

Jahn, Robert G. and Brenda J. Dunne
2008 "Change the Rules!" *Journal of Scientific Exploration*, 22, 2, pp. 193-213.
2011 *Consciousness and the Source of Reality.* Princeton, NJ: ICRL Press.

Kaku, Michio
2008 *Physics of the Impossible: A Scientific Exploration into the World of Phasers, Force Fields, Teleportation and Time Travel.* NY: Doubleday.

Kelly, Edward F., and Emily Williams Kelly
2008 "Where Science and Religion Intersect: The Work of Ian Stevenson," *Journal of Scientific Exploration*, 22, 1, pp. 73-80.

Kelly, Edward F. et al.
2007 *Irreducible Mind: Toward a Psychology for the 21st Century.* Lanham, MD: Rowman & Littlefield Pub., Inc.

Kuhn, Thomas
1962 *The Structure of Scientific Revolutions.* Chicago: U. of Chicago Press.

LaBerge, Stephen

1985 *Lucid Dreaming: The Power of Being Awake and Aware in Your Dreams*. NY: Ballantine Books.

Lester, David

2005 *Is There Life After Death?: An Examination of the Empirical Evidence*. Jefferson, NC: McFarland & Co., Inc.

Lyotard, Jean-Francois

1984 *The Postmodern Condition: A Report on Knowledge*. Minneapolis: U. of Minnesota Press.

Mayer, Elizabeth Lloyd

2007 *Extraordinary Knowing: Science, Skepticism and the Inexplicable Powers of the Human Mind*. NY: Bantam Books.

McClenon, James

1984 *Deviant Science: The Case of Parapsychology*. Philadelphia: The U of Pennsylvania Press.

2002 *Wondrous Healing: Shamanism, Human Evolution, and the Origin of Religion*. DeKalb, IL: Northern Illinois U. Press.

McIntosh, Steve

2007 *Integral Consciousness and the Future of Evolution*. St. Paul, Minnesota: Paragon House.

McTaggart, Lynne

2001 *The Field: The Quest for the Secret Force of the Universe*. NY: HarperCollins Publishers.

Monroe, Robert

1971 *Journeys Out of the Body*. NY: Doubleday.

Moody, Raymond

1975 *Life after Life*. Atlanta: Mockingbird Books.

1993 *Reunions: Visionary Encounters with Departed Loved Ones*. NY: Ballantine.

1999 *The Last Laugh: A New Philosophy of Near-Death Experiences, Apparitions, and the Paranormal*. Charlottesville, VA: Hampton Roads.

Moody, Raymond and Paul Perry

2010 *Glimpses of Eternity*. Guideposts.

Moreman, Christopher

2006 "Mystical Experiences and the Afterlife." In Lance Storm and Michael A. Thalbourne (eds.): *The Survival of Human Consciousness: Essays on the Possibility of Life After Death.* Jefferson, NC: McFarland.

Neppe, Vernon M.

2007 "A Detailed Analysis of an Important Chess Game: Revisiting "Maroczy Versus Korchnoi"," *Journal of the Society for Psychical Research,* 71.3, 888, July, pp. 129-148.

Nesbitt, Mark

1991 *Ghosts of Gettysburg: Spirits, Apparitions, and Haunted Places of the Battlefield.* Gettysburg, PA: Thomas Publications.

Osis, Karlis, and Erlendur Haraldsson

1977 *At the Hour of Death.* NY: Avon.

Postman, Neil

1996 "Social Science as Moral Theology," *Writing Sociology,* 4, 2, fall, pp. 7-8.

Potts, John

2004 "Ghost hunting in the twenty-first century," pp. 211-232 in James Houran (ed.), *From Shaman to Scientist: Essays on Humanity's Search for Spirits.* Lanham, MD: Scarecrow Press.

Radin, Dean

1997 *The Conscious Universe: The Scientific Truth of Psychic Phenomena.* NY: HarperOne.

2006 *Entangled Minds: Extrasensory Experiences in a Quantum Reality.* NY: Paraview Pocket Books.

Rao, K. Ramakrishna

2002 *Consciousness Studies: Cross-Cultural Perspectives.* Jefferson, NC: McFarland & Co, Inc.

Rhine, J.B. (et al.)

1940 *ESP After Sixty Years.* NY: Holt.

Rhine, Louisa E.

1978 "The psi process in spontaneous cases," *Journal of Parapsychology*, 42, March, pp. 20-32.

Roach, Mary

2005 *Spook: Science Tackles the Afterlife*. NY: W.W. Norton & Company.

Rock, Adam J., Julie Beischel and Gary E. Schwartz

2008 "Thematic Analysis of Research Mediums' Experiences of Discarnate Communication," *Journal of Scientific Exploration*, 22, 2, pp. 179-192.

Rogo, D. Scott

1978 *The Haunted House Handbook*. NY: Tempo Books.

1979 The Poltergeist Experience. New York: Penguin.

Rogo, D. Scott, and Raymond Bayless

1980 *Phone Calls from the Dead*. NY: Berkley Books.

Roll, William

1972 *The Poltergeist*. Garden City, NY: Doubleday.

Russell, Ronald

2007 *The Journey of Robert Monroe: From Out-of-Body Explorer to Consciousness Pioneer*. Charlottesville, VA: Hampton Roads.

Sabom, Michael

1998 *Light and Death*. Grand Rapids: Zondervan.

Sagan, Carl

1997A *The Demon-Haunted World: Science as a Candle in the Dark*. NY: Ballantine Books.

1997B *Contact*. NY: Pocket Books.

Saltmarsh, Harold Francis

2004 *The Future and Beyond: Paranormal Foreknowledge and Evidence of Personal Survival from Cross Correspondences*. Charlottesville, VA: Hampton Roads.

Schrodinger, Erwin

1945 *What Is Life?* Cambridge: Cambridge U. Press.

Schwartz, Gary

2002 *The Afterlife Experiments: Breakthrough Scientific Evidence of Life After Death*. NY: Pocket Books.

Schwartz, Gary, and Linda Russek

1999 *The Living Energy Universe*. Charlottesville, VA: Hampton Roads Pub. Co.

Sheldrake, Rupert

2003 *The Sense of Being Stared At and Other Aspects of the Extended Mind*. NY: Crown Publishers.

Simon, Tami (ed.)

2008 *Measuring the Unmeasurable: The Scientific Case for Spirituality*. Boulder, CO: Sounds True.

Stevenson, Ian

1997A *Reincarnation and Biology: A Contribution to the Etiology of Birthmarks and Birth Defects*. Westport, CT: Praeger.

1997B *Where Reincarnation and Biology Intersect*. Westport, CT: Praeger.

2008 (1958) "Scientists with Half-Closed Minds," *Journal of Scientific Exploration*, 22, 1, pp. 132-140.

Storm, Lance and Michael A. Thalbourne (eds.)

2006 *The Survival of Human Consciousness: Essays on the Possibility of Life After Death*. Jefferson, NC: McFarland & Co., Inc.

Sturrock, Peter A.

2007 "The Role of Anomalies in Scientific Research," *Journal of Scientific Exploration*, 21, 2, pp. 241-260.

Tanner, Amy

1994 (1910) *Studies in Spiritualism*. Buffalo, NY: Prometheus Books.

Targ, Russell

2004 *Limitless Mind: A Guide to Remote Viewing and Transformation of Consciousness*. Novato, CA: New World Library.

2010 *Do You See What I See ?: Memoirs of a Blind Biker*. Charlottesville, VA: Hampton Roads.

Targ, Russell and Jane Katra

1998 *Miracles of Mind: Exploring Nonlocal Consciousness and Spiritual Healing*. Novato, CA: New World Library.

Tucker, Jim B., MD

2005 *Life Before Life: A Scientific Investigation of Children's Memories of Previous Lives*. NY: St. Martin's Press.

Tyrrell, G.N.M.

1963 *Apparitions*. NY: Macmillan.

Velmans, Max, and Susan Schneider (eds.)

2007 *The Blackwell Companion to Consciousness*. Malden, MA: Blackwell Pub.

Waggoner, Robert

2009 *Lucid Dreaming: Gateway to the Inner Self*. Needham, MA: Moment Point Press.

Weber, Renee

1986 *Dialogues with Scientists and Sages: The Search for Unity*. London: Routledge and Kegan Paul.

White, K.L.

2008 "Ian Stevenson: Recollections," *Journal of Scientific Exploration*, 22, 1, pp. 16-17.

Wilson, Robert Anton

1991 *The New Inquisition*. Las Vegas: New Falcon Publications.

Index

A

AERU xi, xv, 51

ancestor worship 3-4, 102, 108

anecdotal 8, 10, 24, 38, 49

anomalous xi, xv, 8, 21, 23-4, 30, 33, 35, 37, 43-6, 51

Anomalous Experiences Research Unit xi, xv, 21, 43, 51

anthropology 56

apparition xiii, 2, 40, 57, 77, 87, 102-3, 105-6, 110, 113

apport 119-20

A.R.E. xi, xv

Aronowitz 14, 165

Association for Research and Enlightenment xi, xv

astonishing hypothesis 67, 166

astronomer 28, 31

Atwater xi, 9, 12, 46, 51, 55, 76, 79-81, 151, 165

Avalon xi, 12, 151

Ayurvedic 124

B

Bayless 35, 171

Beauregard 5, 14, 58, 70, 72, 74, 158, 165

Becker 7, 9, 33, 99, 137, 140-1, 150, 165

behaviorism 47, 68

Beischel 51, 171

belief 5, 9, 21-3, 26-7, 31, 38, 41, 121-2, 137, 139, 149-50, 160-1

Benson 75, 165

Berger 159, 165

biology 22, 55-6, 136-7, 155, 172

Blackmore 5, 9, 48, 50, 56, 65, 68-9, 71-4, 80, 85, 165

Blum 57, 165

Boes 123, 165

brain 1, 9, 11, 26-7, 47-8, 50-1, 60-2, 65-8, 70-5, 77-80, 88, 98-9, 101-2, 112-13, 155-6

Braude xi, 17, 22, 35, 42, 77, 80, 83, 115, 119, 131, 157, 166

Buddhism 4, 141

Buddhist 50, 86, 123, 137

Burns xi, 86

C

Carter 7, 11, 66, 70, 166

Castro xi, 44, 52

Caudill 151, 166

Chalmers 48, 67-8, 166

Chamberlain 126-7

chess 128-9, 154, 157, 160-1, 170

Chinese xiii, 3-4, 6, 40-1, 50, 87, 94,
    96, 102-5, 107-9, 128, 131, 137,
    144, 166

Chinese Ghosts xiii, 3, 40, 87, 94, 96,
    102-3, 107, 131, 166

Chomsky 11, 48

Christian 43, 60, 137

clairvoyance 41, 77, 92, 94,
    132-3, 153

collective apparition 87, 103

consciousness xiii-xv, 1-12, 16-18,
    47-51, 53-6, 61-2, 65-86, 88,
    97-102, 104-5, 149-52, 154-8,
    160-3, 165-6, 168-73

Cooley 72

Course in Miracles 43, 60

Crick 56, 67, 71, 166

crisis case 103

Crosby xi, 52, 128, 158

D

Dalai Lama 81

Danielson 151

debunking 14, 21, 80

denial of death 150, 162, 165

dice 40, 53, 115-16, 118-19, 122

Dossey 121

dowsing 37

dream 43, 50-1, 69, 79, 84-91, 103,
    107-8, 153

dreaming 35, 42, 50-1, 84-5, 87-8,
    90, 150, 169, 173

dualism 10, 29, 86, 156, 163

Dunne 53, 118, 168

E

Edwards 26, 136, 166

Eisenbeiss 129, 166

Emmons xiii-xv, 12-14, 21-4, 30-2,
    36-42, 85-90, 94-6, 98-100, 102-4,
    106-8, 114-16, 122-4, 130-2,
    150-2, 158-60

entangled 77-8, 93, 98, 160, 170

epiphenomenon 47-8, 65

ESP xiii, 2-3, 5, 9, 22-5, 31, 34,
    38-40, 77-8, 92-9, 102-5, 107-9,
    125-33, 140-1, 155-6

ethnographic xiv, 27, 32, 49

Evans 98, 104, 108, 110-11, 167

evidential case 103

EVP 44, 111

experiential source theory 102

Exploring the Extraordinary xi

eye-rolling 35, 100, 106, 119, 142

F

First Spiritualist Church of Erie   xi, 117
Fischer   129
Fleming   xi, 24, 40, 115-16
Fontana   22, 49, 167
Forest Temple   132
Fox   5, 77, 167
Fox Sisters   5
frame   xiv-xv, 15, 29, 44, 54-9, 62,
    66-8, 72-5, 94, 99, 104, 110, 119,
    155-7, 162
funding   xi, 13-14, 17, 31, 33, 93, 152

G

Gauld   23, 34, 73, 78, 104, 109-10,
    125-8, 130, 137, 139, 150, 167
Gazzaniga   66, 69, 72, 74, 167
Gehman   xi, 114
Gettysburg   xi, 8, 18, 23, 44, 82, 87,
    110-11, 113, 126-7, 153, 170
ghost   xiii, 2, 27, 39-40, 44, 49-50,
    54, 57, 74, 77, 95, 102, 104-6,
    109-11, 125
ghosts   xiii, 3, 18, 27, 39-41, 44,
    49-50, 57, 65, 74, 87, 92, 101-13,
    126-7, 166-7
Ghosts of Gettysburg   18, 44, 111,
    127, 170
Gilbert   xi, 45, 52

Goffman   54-5, 167
Greeley   5, 97, 167
Greyson   80, 167
Grossman   29, 49-51, 167
Grosso   30, 167
Guided by Spirit   xiii, xv, 89, 96, 114,
    120, 123, 130-1, 142, 167

H

Hafiz   29, 49-51, 167
hallucination   104, 125
Hameroff   73
hard problem   7, 48, 50, 67-8, 81,
    83, 166
harp   37-8
Hassler   129, 166
haunting   103, 108-10
healing   30, 43, 45, 79, 100, 106,
    112-13, 121-4, 130, 133, 150-1,
    155-6, 158-9, 169, 173
Heath   53, 168
hoax   41, 114, 125
Home   119
Hong Kong   3-4, 49, 87, 96, 103,
    128, 137
Horgan   8, 11, 23, 66, 72, 168
humanities   4, 31, 94
Husveth   xi, 44, 111
Hyman   25
Hynek   28

I

ideological 9, 30
Institute of Noetic Sciences xi, xv, 17, 131
IONS xi, xv, 17, 43, 131, 158

J

Jacobson 66, 168
Jahn 28, 32, 53, 118, 155, 168
James xi, 7, 29, 57, 94, 122, 157, 165, 169-70
Jeannerod 70
Jefferson 61, 144, 169-70, 172

K

Kaku 27-8, 32, 118, 168
Katra 92, 121, 158, 172
Kelly 15, 29, 48, 57, 73, 76, 168
Klipper 75, 165
Korchnoi 129, 154, 160-1, 170
Kuhn 30, 33, 55, 168

L

LaBerge 50-1, 77, 79, 84-8, 150, 168
LD 50-1, 85-8, 150
Lee 96
Lester 25-6, 169
levitation 35, 113-14
Lily Dale xi, 81, 106, 117-18, 132-3

Lily Dale Assembly xi
Lipton 70
lucid dreaming 42, 50, 84, 88, 90, 150, 169, 173
Lyotard 58, 169

M

mainstream xiii, 3-8, 11, 13-17, 25, 30, 33-5, 37, 42, 47, 53, 58, 66, 73, 136-7
Maroczy 129, 160-1, 170
materialist 11, 15, 31, 37, 67, 115, 159
Mayer 4, 9, 17, 24-5, 28, 30, 32, 35, 37-9, 43, 93, 99, 118, 169
McClenon xi, 7, 30, 32-4, 38, 58, 94, 102, 122, 157, 169
McIntosh 61-2, 169
McNab v, xi, 81
McTaggert 123
meme 72
Metcalf xi, 21-2, 45, 52
methodology 10, 15, 24, 27, 30, 32, 44, 51-2, 54, 57, 66, 74, 118, 142, 155
Miller xi, 43, 151
Monroe xi, xv, 9, 12, 43, 45, 77, 79, 144, 150-1, 169, 171
Monroe Institute xi, xv, 9, 12, 43, 45, 144, 150
Moody 10, 28-9, 35, 49, 58, 77, 81, 169

Moreman   4, 170

mystic   59-60, 143

N

Native American   61, 82

Natural Bridge   143

natural science   31

NDE   10, 25, 49, 56, 58, 60, 76,
78-81, 89

near-death experience   167

Neppe   129, 170

Nesbitt   xi, 18, 44, 111, 170

neurophysiology   48, 77

neuroscience   xiv, 1, 9, 11, 18,
48, 66-7, 69, 73, 77, 87, 97,
152, 155-6

New Age   8, 16-17, 66-7, 138,
152, 166

New Spirituality   17, 152, 167

nonmaterialist   11, 58, 67

normal science   11, 13-14, 16, 28,
30-1, 33, 35, 54, 57, 68, 95,
142, 152

O

OBE   10, 76, 78-80, 99

objective   48-9, 51, 53, 61, 66, 68, 76,
81, 83, 131, 149, 155, 158

objectivity   xiii, 52

obsession   126-7

orthodox   29-30, 134

Ouija board   113

P

Palladino   119

paradigm   11, 33, 40, 66, 163

paranormal   xiii-xv, 4-11, 13-14, 17-18,
27-9, 40-5, 92-4, 97-100, 102-5,
111-13, 120-3, 137-8, 149-50,
159-60, 165-9

paranormal investigator   18

paraphysical   104-5

parapsychology   xiv, 5-7, 15-17, 28,
30-4, 44, 56-7, 73, 115, 121, 138,
155-8, 168-9, 171

participatory science   52

past-life   138-43, 157

PEAR   28, 53

Penelope   iv, xiii-xv, 2, 4, 6, 8, 96,
116-18, 120, 126-8, 130-2, 134-5,
142, 158-62, 166

Penrose   73

Perry   81, 169

Pert   71-2

phenomenological   34, 41, 51-3, 81,
131, 168

philosophy   xiv, 12, 16-17, 42, 48, 55,
59, 69, 115, 157, 166, 169

physical effect   49, 104-6, 119, 121

physics   9, 11-12, 16, 27, 40, 55, 66,
77, 98-9, 104, 123, 152, 155-7,
160, 165

PK 8, 35, 40, 53, 79, 93, 100, 106-8,
    112-13, 115-19, 122-3, 156-7,
    159, 168
placebo 14, 122
poll 136-7
poltergeist 6, 106-7, 113, 117, 171
possession 6, 113, 126-7, 140
Postman 32, 170
Potts 27, 170
prayer 17, 121, 151
precognition 43, 87, 92, 94
precognitive 42-3, 87, 95
Prime xi
Princess Ileana 134
psi xiv, 2, 7, 11, 23-5, 31, 34-5, 38,
    43, 50, 67, 73, 93-8, 156-8, 160
psychic teeth 120
psychic watch 117
psychokinesis 8, 27, 53, 93, 113,
    115, 166
psychology xiv, 7, 16-18, 22, 24, 31,
    38, 40, 47, 49, 55-6, 93-4, 115-16,
    155, 167-8

Q

qualia 68
quantum physics 11-12, 66, 77, 98-9,
    104, 123, 152, 155-7, 160

R

Rademacher xi, 9, 12, 45, 151
Radin xi, 9, 17, 22-3, 43, 48, 66-7, 72,
    74, 93-5, 98, 121, 130, 155-6, 158
Rao 4, 9, 47, 50, 55, 65-6, 73, 170
Rauber xi, 44, 111
reiki 43, 121, 123-4
reincarnation xiii, 2, 13, 15, 22, 26-7,
    34, 57-8, 80, 99, 108, 136-43,
    150, 161-2, 172
religion xiv, 3, 8, 12, 15, 22, 29-30,
    43, 49, 57, 142, 149-50, 152,
    162, 167-9
remote viewing 12, 17, 25, 39, 42, 46,
    58, 77-8, 89, 92-3, 95, 97, 104,
    130-1, 151
retrocognition 110
Reynolds 80
Rhine xi, 24-5, 28, 32, 40, 92-4, 97,
    116, 170
Roach 16, 28, 171
Rock 51, 171
Rogo 5-6, 35, 97, 105-6, 109, 113,
    123, 171
Roll 106, 111, 152, 167, 171
Roll Your Own Religion 152, 167
Rollans 129
Roman Catholic 6, 113, 134
Roney-Dougal xi
Russek 110, 172

Russell   xi, 17, 29, 39, 42-3, 58-9,
    62, 78-9, 92, 99, 122, 128-9, 150,
    154, 171-2

.

S

Sabom 80, 171
Sagan 62, 137-8, 171
Saltmarsh 127, 171
Schlitz 121
Schneider 67, 70, 166, 173
Schroedinger 66, 68
Schwartz 9, 51, 95, 110, 131,
    150, 171-2
scientism 29
self 1-2, 4, 51, 61, 69-74, 84, 86,
    88-9, 100, 104-5, 116, 132,
    150, 173
SETI 13, 58
Sheldrake 100-1, 105, 172
Sidgwick 57, 127
Simon 45, 70-1, 121, 151, 165, 172
skepticism 14, 21-2, 25-7, 29, 33,
    37-8, 41, 93, 96, 118, 136, 169
Skinner 47-8, 65
social control 28, 39, 42, 93
social science xiii, 40, 158, 170
Society for Psychical Research 24,
    92, 127, 129, 166-7, 170
Society for Scientific Exploration xi,
    xiv, 1, 15, 33, 43, 51, 142

sociologist xiii-xiv, 3, 23, 40, 49, 51-2,
    54-6, 68-9, 130, 135, 149, 154,
    159, 162
sociology xi, xiii-xv, 23, 32, 45, 47, 54,
    56, 72-3, 142, 149, 155, 158-9,
    165, 170
spirit medium   xiii, xv, 4, 32, 45, 52,
    82, 87, 94, 96, 114, 125, 128,
    131, 154
spirit mediums   xiii, 3-4, 32, 37, 41-2,
    45, 51-3, 58, 85-7, 92, 99, 127-8,
    130-1, 150, 157-8
spirit mediumship   xiii, xv, 2, 5-6, 9,
    13, 17, 41, 45, 52, 94-5, 97, 125,
    130-1, 156
spiritual 5-6, 9, 12, 15, 17, 26, 45-7,
    56, 59-61, 73-4, 76, 112-13,
    121-2, 156, 159
Spiritualism 12, 23, 56-7, 92, 149,
    158, 172
spirituality xiv, 8-9, 17, 22, 45, 49, 62,
    151-2, 167-8, 172
Sprinkle xi, 35, 138, 142
Stevenson 15-16, 22, 26-7, 30,
    34, 57, 80, 126, 136-42, 150,
    167-8, 172-3
Storm 5, 170, 172
Sturrock 31, 33, 172
subjective xiii, 9, 12, 34, 41, 45-53,
    61, 65-8, 70-1, 81, 83, 85, 88,
    97, 155
subjectivity 47, 68
superskepticism 21, 93

survival   1-7, 53-5, 73, 79-80, 83, 99,
    102-3, 108, 125, 128-31, 135-7,
    156, 160-2, 165-8, 170-2
symbolic interaction   55

T

table-tipping   41, 114-15
Takei   xi
Tanner   22-3, 172
Taoism   86
Targ   xi, 5, 17, 25, 29, 34, 39,
    42-3, 58-9, 62, 78, 92, 121-3,
    127-9, 172
telepathy   23, 27, 48, 87, 92, 94,
    132-4, 160
Templeton Foundation   15, 57
Terry   xi, 73-4
Thalbourne   5, 170, 172
theological   77
theology   55-6, 170
TMI   xv, 9, 12, 43, 45-6, 150-1
Tucker   138-40, 173
Tyrrell   105, 173

U

UFO   13-14, 21, 23, 28, 31, 35, 39,
    42, 58, 95, 102, 138, 141, 160

V

Velmans   67, 70, 166, 173

W

Waggoner   xi, 42, 51, 77, 79, 84-8,
    150, 173
Wagner   71
Watson   47-8, 65, 68
Weber   9, 173
White   15-16, 173
Wilson   8, 29, 173
Wooffitt   xi, 43, 51

X

xenoglossy   128